Jim Seymour's

On The Road

The Portable Computing Bible

BY

JIM SEYMOUR

EDITED BY

NORA SEYMOUR

Brady Publishing

Published by Brady Publishing
A division of Prentice Hall Computer Publishing
15 Columbus Circle
New York, NY 10023

Manufactured in the United States of America

10 9 8 7 6 5 4 3

ISBN: 0-13-512294-5

Dedication

For my favorite little laptop, Graham.

Trademarks

Limits of Liability and Disclaimer

Contents

II. Hitting the Road

Preface

Ever notice something odd about those portable-PC ads you see in the computer magazines, in airline magazines, on the illuminated posters lining airport concourses? Ever notice how they always show someone using a notebook or laptop PC in . . . well, a vacuum?

These ads would have us believe that anyone savvy enough to use a portable PC need carry nothing else with them when they travel. Well, an umbrella, maybe. Or a snazzy Burberry raincoat. Maybe a nice alligator-skin attaché case. And, just maybe, a fresh shirt or blouse, tucked away somewhere. But that's it.

Where do these people put their airline tickets, I wonder? Their itineraries? *Official Airline Guides*? Pictures of their families? The reports, memoranda, contracts, and other work they'll be handling en route? Product literature from their companies? A magazine or two and this morning's *Wall Street Journal?* Pencils, pens, markers, business cards? A little dictating machine? A cellular phone, maybe? An address book? A Filofax? And where's the PC's battery-charger/power supply? Its power cord? An extra battery? A phone cable for the PC's modem? Some floppy disks?

Once, I dumped out my travelling case and weighed everything I carried along with my notebook PC, minus the PC itself. The PC turned out to be less than a third of the total weight and maybe a sixth of the bulk.

Forget the ads. If you travel with a business machine—*any* business machine—you carry along all the paraphernalia of that machine, too. Plus all the traditional stuff you've always carried. Start using a portable PC and you don't just carry a PC when you travel; you carry a PC kit. Actually, a *business* kit.

Which is the whole point of laptops and notebooks—a point that sometimes gets lost in gee-whizzy discussions of their features. Notebook PCs won't make you taller, smarter, younger, more handsome or more beautiful. They certainly *can* make you richer, help you use your work day better and thus have more time for your family and friends, help you rise through the corporate hierarchy, maybe even help you go out and start a corporate hierarchy of your own.

But to make sense of them, we have to see them as *business tools.* Period.

I don't love PCs; I love what they can do for me. So do you, judging from the mountains of reader mail I get when I write a column about keeping computers in perspective.

And yet, the gee-whizzy stuff counts. We all like using the newest, fastest, smallest toys. We like the convenience of powerful portable computers—flat, black boxes that are far more powerful than the desktop PCs of a couple of years ago, and more powerful, for a single user's purposes, than many of the hulking minicomputers of four or five years ago.

But threading a path between the useful and the merely glitzy can be tough. It's incredibly easy to buy a good notebook PC these days—just look for a 386SX machine from a vendor you've heard of—but it can be very hard to buy the right one *for your purposes.*

Hence this book.

I wasn't interested in writing a book about the portable computers of yesterday, because they were full of compromises. You gave up too much to take a computer on the road to make the notion very interesting. While I've been carrying portable PCs on business trips since the early 1980s, I didn't much like the pain/gain return in those days.

Now, portable PCs—truly portable PCs, six- and seven-pound wonders I can slip into my beloved old Hartmann attaché case when necessary—give me essentially everything I get from my desktop PC. There are still compromises, to be sure, but *none of them matter in the context of a business tool.* If I forsake a big, colorful CRT monitor at my desk, in return I get a bright, sharp, color LCD display that I can use anywhere. If I give up the fast 330 MB hard disk on my desktop PC—a system a friend once said looked as if was powerful enough to launch missiles—I get a fast 80 MB disk, doubled in capacity to something over 160 MB with Stacker, that I can use anywhere.

Are those burdensome compromises? Not for me. Do they diminish the power of that notebook PC versus the desktop as a business tool? You've got to be kidding.

To the contrary, clients are often wowed when I pop open my seven-pound notebook and bring up a series of graphs in dazzling active-matrix color. *How do you do that?* they ask.

That's a business tool. And that's what this book is all about.

Jim Seymour

Austin

May 17, 1992

I.

PORTABLE PCS: THE LOGICAL EVOLUTION

Sorting Out Portable PCs

A taxonomy of kinds of portable PCs, from the early suitcase-sized machines to today's incredible palmtop gizmos, can be a big help in sorting out what you have and what you may want to buy.

If you're already deep into using a notebook or laptop PC, you may want to skip these first few chapters; they're meant to give context for the newcomer and to prepare the experienced user plunging back into the market. But before you skip ahead, consider: if you've been burned once on buying a portable PC, and if you recall Santayana's warning about those who forget history having to relive it, then you'll want to read this first part before jumping in again.

Laptops versus Notebooks

This one's easy, but I'm going to irritate the heck out of a lot of readers with it: If you're going out to buy a portable PC today, you want a notebook PC, not a laptop. And if you already *have* a laptop, consider whether it's time to pass it along to someone else and start looking for a notebook.

OK, all you happy laptop PC owners—yeah, including the ones who just bought their machines six months ago—sit down and be quiet. I'm not attacking your judgement or your intelligence. I've bought a couple of laptops in my time, too. But today, notebooks are, if you'll forgive the expression, where it's at.

Unless you fit into one of the categories described in "Types of Users, Types of Needs" for which a lot more computing power than is presently available in notebooks is needed, stay with a notebook. And if you like the size and weight of notebooks better than the size and weight of laptops—who wouldn't?—but *do* need more power, consider waiting a few months: notebooks will probably be powerful enough for you by then.

Notebook PCs can be tossed into briefcases and attache cases; laptops usually cannot. Notebooks can easily be stashed in a protective nest of clothing inside a suitcase when you're travelling and for whatever reason simply must check your PC; laptops take up a *lot* more space. Notebooks have all the latest technological gains; laptops, whose time on the cutting edge of PC technology is well past, do not. Notebooks give long battery life, thanks to newly developed power-saving chips and techniques, plus better battery systems; laptops do not.

And though they're smaller and lighter, notebook PCs are often tougher than much more substantial laptop PCs; the ruggedness of hard disks, displays and other key components has improved greatly in the last couple of years.

All that said, laptop PCs are pretty incredible machines. When they were first introduced, they were real marvels: how *did* Toshiba pack all the power of a hulking IBM PC AT desktop computer into that dinky little T3100 laptop? If you have one and like it, you should keep using it as long as it meets your needs.

But you'd better not read the ads for today's notebooks. Because when you start noticing that you can get a machine half the size and weight, with maybe three times the computing power of your laptop and half again its battery life (your laptop *does* work on batteries, doesn't it. . . ?), for under $2,000, you're going to start reaching for your check-signing pen. . .

‘Subnotebooks’: The Next Generation

When the first true notebook PCs appeared—the ones that were maybe an inch-and-a-half thick, about the size of a piece of typing paper, and weighed seven or eight pounds—industry gurus and prognosticators were in heaven. Portable PCs would never get any better than this, they said; they'd never get smaller or lighter; and besides, this was as small as any real computer *needed* to be.

A little while later, the Poquet palmtop PC came along and confirmed their beliefs. Clearly the Poquet showed everything that was wrong with the idea of smaller-than-notebooks personal computers: a sorry, squinched-up keyboard; a dim display with tiny, nearly illegible characters; mediocre performance; and so on. It was a compromised-out machine in their view—true enough—and that was that.

What they missed was the critical evolutionary step between the notebooks and the palm-tops: a brand-new class of machines we've begun calling “subnotebooks.” They missed it, of course, because this evolution stepped out of the expected chronology: the Poquet palmtop appeared long before the first of the subnotebooks and looked for a while like the next step down. Thank God it wasn't.

"Subnotebook" is an unfortunate name, because it suggests subnotebook *performance* as well as subnotebook size. Yet the very first generation of subnotebooks are remarkably close in power and functionality to many of today's best-selling notebook PCs—and the next generation of these little machines is going to be even better.

If you were, and maybe still are, skeptical about the usefulness and probable success of subnotebooks, you're in good company. I felt that way too, and the feeling was reinforced as I saw prototype after dreary prototype of subnotebooks-to-come which served no need I had seen in the computer marketplace. They were technologically a generation behind, and while, sure, they were smaller and lighter, they typically fell beneath the threshold of pain in usability: what would we *do* with these half-computers?

Something happened between those first prototypes and the emergence of real subnotebooks in mid-1992. I think PC manufacturers eager to play in this game realized that PC users were simply too smart to be fooled by half-a-loaf designs. They'd gotten used to the power and convenience of notebook PCs, and while they'd love to pack all that notebook power into smaller and lighter machines, they weren't about to give up the functionality they'd learned they needed.

Put simply, PCs had become too important to them as business tools to revert to toy machines—no matter how tiny and cute.

Let me say this plainly: I think subnotebooks are the wave of the mid-term future. While today's "subs" often fall a little shy of the performance and versatility we want in general-purpose business computers, they're already great tools for frequent travellers. With remarkably large hard disks (to 120 MB and, soon, more) uncompromised 386SX-level power (in the form of low-power 386SL variations on the SX theme), and surprisingly good keyboards, they are all the computer many of us need.

Where they fall down, at least so far, is in display quality. Delivering a useful battery life—which means at least two to two-and-a-half hours per user-changeable battery—has meant forsaking the bright, backlit screens many of us have come to expect from notebook PCs. First-wave subnotebooks rely on reflective LCD displays which, though they are a big improvement over the reflective, non-backlit displays of just a couple of years ago, still aren't in a league with their backlit counterparts. Lower-power cold-cathode backlighting systems combined with higher-output nickel-hydride batteries will bring backlit screens to subnotebooks before long, and when these machines cross that Rubicon, there'll be no stopping them.

The biggest worry I had about subnotebooks—a problem I had at first thought would keep them always beneath the minimum acceptable level of usability—was their keyboard size. Clearly, I thought, notebook keyboards had done all the shrinking and rearranging a few tens of millions of other PC users and I could stand.

So I was very pleased when the first subnotebooks came to market, because they managed to squeeze a little more fat out of the keyboard without squeezing out any important features. I want a subnotebook keyboard with standard desktop-PC-keyboard spacing between keys, a reasonable vertical displacement when I hit a key, and even a little clickiness (or "audible feedback," in product-brochure-speak).

The best subnotebook designs I've seen so far include a very usable keyboard, a large hard disk, 386SL power, almost three hours of battery life . . . and that mediocre, reflective LCD display. No more working all night to the sounds of snoring seatmates in darkened cabins on red-eye flights, the glow from my computer screen providing just enough light for a hunt-and-peck typist like me to see the keyboard. All of these machines need a reasonably well-lit environment to deliver an acceptable screen image.

On the other hand, most of them are smaller than a hardbound book, weigh about three pounds, and make a perfectly acceptable writing and electronic-mailing companion on trips where I just don't plan to do heavy-duty computing.

I haven't retired my notebooks yet, and I don't expect to for some time. But I've seen the future—and it almost fits in my coat pocket.

Pen PCs: Portables with a Difference

It's impossible to talk about portable PCs today without also talking about so-called pen PCs, also known as "slate" PCs. While they are indisputably portable—in fact, they make little or no sense for use at a desk—they are such a different breed, and for now at least are intended for such different uses, that's it's all too easy for even the savvy PC user to get sidetracked by the notion of adopting a pen PC as his or her portable.

All pen PCs are based on input from a stylus, or inkless pen, with which the user marks on a large, flat screen. Most pen PCs are about the size of large clipboards; the screen usually takes up about 75 – 90 percent of the surface. Inside the four-to-six-pound case lurk a microprocessor, hard disk, RAM, and all the other components of a portable computer.

Because pen PCs are so clearly intended for stylus input, many users have tended to focus on handwriting recognition capabilities as the acid test of the machines' usefulness. While some level of handwriting recognition is built into virtually every pen PC (or pen-PC operating system), and being able to scribble notes onscreen is certainly part of what they're about, seeing pen PCs primarily as devices that replace typed input with handwritten input misses the point.

Some industry seers have suggested that executives' famous fear of keyboards—a disease which actually disappeared from most of the known world in the late 1980s—makes them prime candidates for pen

PCs. I don't doubt that we'll see executives using pen PCs before long, but once again, that misses the point, because it still focuses on replacing keyboard input with handwritten input, via a unit's stylus.

In fact, pen PCs are intended for a very different kind of computing. And in that role, they will prove to be among the most important forces in business computing since the introduction of the IBM PC in 1981.

In their first years in the market, pen PCs will be used primarily by people who need sketch-level graphical input, and by people who need to manage a database of information without typing in commands, data, and queries. Here again, the gurus missed the boat: many have said that pen PCs will be used almost entirely by blue-collar workers, such as route drivers and deliverymen for snack-foods companies and bakeries. Yes, that *will* be an important part of the pen-PC business—and in the process, we'll sweep whole new classes of workers into the business of using personal computers.

But to envision pen PCs only as electronic clipboards is dead wrong, because an awful lot of professionals will be using them as well. Let's look at both kinds of users. In the process, notice how different these uses are from how we presently see portable computers used in business—and how different, probably, they are from your needs as a general-purpose business-computer user.

Since PC-industry gurus like to characterize those famous snack-company route drivers as the primary users of pen PCs, let's start with them. They're actually a pretty good example of one kind of pen-PC use—but only one kind.

Charlie Cheesechip starts his day by picking up his pen PC at the distribution center and carrying it out to his delivery truck. Snack-foods manufacturers long ago turned their drivers into "route managers," and the term is much more than merely an honorific intended to make delivery men happy with their lot in life.

Today's drivers/route managers do inventory checks at every location, then rearrange the merchandise in grocers' display racks to straighten out all the packages you and I put in the wrong place—and to make sure that in this highly competitive business they don't lose an inch of precious shelf space.

They carry records on the optimum inventory levels for every product, in every size package, for each location, and also have data on the right product-mix within the company's line, which often varies greatly from location to location based on the demographics of the typical shoppers at those locations.

By regularly restocking the shelves to those predetermined optimum-inventory levels, the driver has available invaluable, site-specific information on what is and isn't moving—early retail buying-trend data worth a fortune to the company's product planners.

If managing all this data and making it available throughout the company on short notice sounds like a perfect job for a personal computer—well, it is. But until now, lugging a typical portable PC into the store was simply out of the question: typing data was too time-consuming and too error prone . . . and where would the driver *put* the PC while he was working with it?

Enter pen PCs.

Before Charlie picks up his PC each morning, it has been downloaded with all the information needed for that day's work: stores to be visited, the most efficient order in which to visit them, complete inventory-level information about each, and customer-pricing data. All this can be updated overnight, each night, so the company can make, say, pricing or product-mix changes—or delay deliveries to slow-paying outlets—on 24 hours' notice.

At each location, Charlie goes through the usual manual rearranging of the shelves and counting inventory; PCs can't help with that yet. As he works, he enters the number of packages of each product and size he finds in the pen PC. Rather than typing—or writing—the data, he simply touches digits in three parallel rows of numbers from 0 to 9. Thus he can enter a tally of up to 999 packages of every product. He doesn't enter product names or sizes, either: they appear, in succession, in the same order they appear from top to bottom in the store racks, in a scrolling window on the pen PC's screen. He simply taps the stylus on the name of the product he's registering, then taps the stylus on the digits for the product count. As he touches each succeeding product name, data for the previous one is entered.

When he finishes the inventory, the computer compares each product's count to the desirable-inventory-level data stored on the pen PC's hard disk, then prepares and displays a list—again, in shelf order—of items and quantities to be put on the shelf. A trip or two to the truck, the merchandise is moved to the shelves, and Charlie is through.

If absolutely up-to-the-minute sales data is required, Charlie can tap another spot on the pen PC's display when he returns to the truck after completing his work at each site; a radio modem sends that store's data through a wireless packet-switching network, and into the company's mainframes. If daily updating is sufficient, he simply plugs the machine into a rack-like device when he returns to the distribution center at the end of the day, and the data from all drivers' machines is gathered, sorted, and passed along to the mainframes via modem each night.

During that same overnight log-on, any price changes, adjustments to desirable inventory levels (to accommodate seasonal sales demands, such as Fourth of July weekends' blockbuster sales of chips), or messages regarding tomorrow's deliveries are downloaded to the pen PC. Drivers can also get from these automatic nightly downloads current information about their performance: gross sales, commissions, standings in sales contests, etc. And the company can use the pen-PC connection for a kind of instant, daily electronic employee newsletter, updating workers, for example, on changes in benefit programs. Personal messages can also be passed both ways; these workers are now tightly coupled to the company's existing electronic-mail system, which has a gateway to the communication server managing the overnight downloads and uploads.

All that, you'll note, was accomplished without any feats of computerized handwriting recognition. Because when a PC user is operating within a known universe of variables—a list of accounts, customer credit histories, product lists and prices, etc.—it's much faster and less error-prone to enter data from what are called "pick lists," than to write (or type) entries and queries. Of course, information can always be entered in handwritten form as well, if necessary, to be decoded and converted to an ASCII-character stream by the pen PC.

Now Charlie is squarely in the mainstream of personal computer users in the company. He's actively managing those accounts of his; he's freed of a torrent of pencil-and-paper work; and he's always working with current, up-to-the-minute information. So is the company: no more rooms full of data-entry clerks trying to decipher week-old handwritten scrawls, no more missed communications on price changes, no more stale inventory on the shelves or in the warehouse.

The company and the route manager are both able to turn on a dime to respond to market changes. And the information captured by the driver's use of a PC becomes truly strategic: a basis for managing the *business,* not merely managing the deliveries.

With that kind of power in hand—literally—it's easy to see why some have focused only on that kind of application for pen PCs. But the impact on other kinds of PC users will be at least as great.

Nora Lloyd Wright, let us imagine, is an architect and space-planner. She specializes in designing office layouts that speed work-flow, promote individual productivity, and simply make people feel good about coming to work.

She uses a powerful desktop PC with AutoCAD for most of her work. But over the years she has often been frustrated by both the difficulties of involving managers and workers in client companies in the process of redesigning their workspaces and by the expensive delays in getting approval for her designs as she kept returning time and again to the drawing board, and later to her desktop PC, to turn out yet another set of revisions. She wanted to make the process more interactive and more immediate.

So she turned to a pen PC. Now she downloads her nearly final floorplans onto the pen PC, then visits the job site with it in hand. If it's an existing office she's redesigning, she sits down with the appropriate department manager for an overall review of her plans, then visits with individual workers to discuss their needs and show them her ideas right on the screen of the pen PC. Because people see what's coming before the changes are made, they have a chance to give their input. Wright can integrate their ideas into the plans, trying A versus B as they watch. And because they now feel a part of the process, both managers and office workers are much less likely to be unhappy with the results: they have, in the vernacular, some "ownership" in the redesign.

Wright also finishes the job far faster, because the final sign-offs come sooner, thanks to clients' chances to work out their inevitable "but what if . . . ?" questions with her without going to blueprints for each revision.

If it's new, unoccupied space she's designing, she takes a manager and a couple of workers along to the empty floor of the office building and uses the pen PC's screen to show them the possibilities as they walk around the building itself. Again: ownership, satisfaction, quicker completion.

And happier clients.

It's clear that professionals in many areas, who have to (or like to) deal with their work in graphical form, are going to be using pen PCs. And because the essence of the pen PC is portability, pen PCs are going to widen our definition of the term "portable computer."

All this is very different from many PC users' first impressions of how pen PCs might be used. Very few of us will use them as replacements for keyboard-driven computers; it's just too slow to enter much word-processing text, or many numbers and formulas in a big spreadsheet model, by hand. And though we've seen at least one pen PC so far—Momenta's keyboard-plus-stylus machine—which tries an unlikely straddle by keeping a foot in both worlds, pen PCs are going to be just that: *pen* PCs. (Many will also include a connector for a standard PC keyboard, because once in a while it may be useful to be able to enter a lot of text into the machine. It's cheap and easy to make the keyboard connection, so to speak, so vendors will likely make that a standard feature.)

And while handwriting recognition is an important part of the pen PC's bag of tricks, it's far from the most important. Size, weight and cost—the big three in all portable-PC design—will be far more important than the perfection of a given machine's ability to decipher handwriting.

You can see why I said I don't think you're going to want a pen PC as your primary portable computer, or even your only computer. Unless you fall into one of these groups for which pen PCs are so perfectly suited, a conventional machine makes a lot more sense.

But keep your eye on pen PCs: they're an important step in expanding the notion of "personal computing" beyond our traditional expectations.

Palmtops, Pocketables

The law of diminishing returns always gets you in the end. Basically, that's how I feel about so-called palmtop and pocketable PCs. Two observations: Yes, it can be done. And who cares?

Two palmtop PC designs have dominated the field so far. The Poquet PC, the first entry, was well ahead of its time when introduced in 1989. It will run DOS, and—if you can figure out how to fit them in memory—it will run some DOS programs. Of course, you may not be able to see them on its dim screen. And you may not be able to get accurate input into the machine, thanks to its dwarf keyboard. But yes, it does run DOS—real, honest-to-Bill Gates DOS—and if you like to buy products that prove something can be done, even if it makes no sense to do the thing that way—remember the singing dog?—line up right away for a Poquet.

Before it's discontinued for lack of interest.

The second important entrant in the palmtop-PC derby is in many ways more interesting, if even more limited. Hewlett-Packard's 95LX is a calculator-sized wonder which has real, honest-to-Jim Manzi Lotus 1-2-3 built-into its permanent memory. You can build 1-2-3 worksheets in the 95LX, then upload them to a DOS PC through a cable or a clever infrared link; and you can similarly download 1-2-3 models constructed on your desktop PC to the 95LX. This is a customized version of 1-2-3 release 2.2, and it's been designed to work reasonably well with the 95LX's 16-line by 40-character display.

With an 8088 CPU chip, MS-DOS 3.2 in ROM, and 512 KB of user RAM available, the 95LX can also run some other DOS programs, if you can load them and fit them into its memory. But they may not make much sense on that fraction-of-a-real-screen display: how'd you like to do your work with three-quarters of your PC's screen blacked-out?

The machine's other tricks are less interesting. It has feeble notepad, scheduling, and communications capabilities, but it does have a pretty good calculator. If you've long wanted a powerful financial calculator, but can never remember how to use the Reverse Polish Notation of HP's industry-standard 12C pocket calculator, buy a 95LX: it will walk you through many of the same calculations effortlessly.

Despite all that, for most of us, the appeal of the HP 95LX lies in its built-in version of the all-time best-selling spreadsheet program. If putting 1-2-3 in your pocket appeals, run out and buy a 95LX right away. (You might also sit down and write me a note someday, explaining why a pocket version of 1-2-3 is so important for you. I've been unable to find any 95LX 1-2-3 users who can explain their fondness for running Lotus spreadsheets on the machine.)

We'll see other pocketable PCs, and they'll gradually get more useful. But the limitations on display size and legibility and keyboard size demonstrated by the Poquet and the H-P 95LX aren't likely to be overcome sufficiently to pull this type of machine above the threshold of pain for most of us. It isn't technology that's failing us, but the size of our fingers and the acuity of our vision. Silicon Valley is unlikely to be able to fix those problems.

Palmtops and pocketables are cute, clever, and attract a lot of attention. But they won't do much for your productivity.

Sharp Wizards, Casio BOSSes, Etc.

The electronics discounters and office-supply stores are full these days of cute little things that look like they want to be computers. They have names like Wizard and BOSS, and they can be fun to play with. They may even make adequate schedulers or calculators, depending on your work habits and preferences. But they aren't going to do your computing for you, and you should avoid getting side-tracked by them.

I'm a sucker for little electronic gizmos that promise to improve my life. Indeed, I have a drawerful of them, representing maybe two grand I've wasted over the years. Successive models have gotten smaller, cuter, and more powerful. But in the end they've all proved only marginally useful at best. And they've all gone into that drawer.

In fact, I'm such a sucker for the idea of these things that I *keep* buying them and trying them for a couple of weeks. Then I open that drawer . . . .

Of the lot, the various Sharp Wizards and Casio BOSSes are probably the best. If you really want to keep your daily appointment schedule on a pocketable electronic gizmo, and want to carry a limited-size phone-number list with you in electronic form, then maybe you'll find them useful. The Sharp and Casio units, at least, proved reliable if still not very useful.

But I should tell you that of all my friends who've also bought and tried to use them—and this is a pretty gung-ho, pro-technology bunch, disposed to put up with all sorts of inconveniences most people would never consider—none still use them.

Like me, they have this drawer . . . .

The Short Half-life of Portable PCs

Physicists talk about the half-life of unstable nuclear elements: the rapid decay of the element as it seeks a more stable form, with its radioactivity falling by half every so many months. Something like that applies to notebook and laptop PCs, too, and it's important to understand that phenomenon before you jump into the game.

Most corporate PC-buyers recognize that desktop PCs have a useful life of about three years. That doesn't match the depreciation rate approved by the Internal Revenue Service, which is still stuck, foolishly, at five years. But in practice, if you make a smart buy on a desktop PC, you'll get a machine which, for about three years, will be reasonably up-to-date—certainly in the last half of that life, behind the cutting edge of computer technology, but still very useful.

(Many companies, and many individuals, continue to operate PCs long after that period, of course; there are lots of wheezing IBM PCs and PC-XTs out there, a decade or more old and still in service. We're not talking about machines burning out after three years, but rather, machines which have become so thoroughly superseded, technically, by later designs that they begin to compromise your ability to do the work you want to do with them.)

For notebook and laptop PCs, that useful-life curve is only about 18 months long. And in fact, most savvy corporate PC managers plan notebook PC purchases on the basis of cost-recovery over that period of time, or less. They know that in 18 to 24 months, notebook PCs will have advanced sufficiently that many of their users will begin looking longingly at new models. And these managers will, too, as they become eager to move new, higher-level applications onto their employees' PCs.

None of this means you necessarily have to buy a new machine every 18 months—in fact, few of us do—but only that you should avoid buying on the hind-side of this curve, lest you get left even further behind as the leading edge of technology moves on. Buy a machine near the end of its short life near the front of the pack, and you may get clobbered by how quickly it becomes effectively (if hardly functionally) obsolete.

No one says you have to use state-of-the-art equipment—in "Notetakers," for example, in the next part of this book, I recommend thoroughly obsolete 12 MHz 80286-based notebook PCs for some uses—but in your assessment of whether or not you're getting a good deal, remember that very short half-life of portable PCs.

Then buy, and plan, accordingly.

The Windows Question

We can't go on to consider who uses PCs, and how, with an eye towards choosing the right one, without first addressing a question that fundamentally shapes your decision: *Do you use Windows?*

If you do, forget everything you read in the rest of this book about portable PCs of modest power. If you're a Windows user, or about to become one, you want at least the power of a 20 MHz 386SX or 386SL PC. With a 60 MB or larger hard disk. And you want to rethink the color issue as well (see "Do You Really Need Color?" in *Buying Smart: Notebooks for the '90s)*.

Windows, in its present incarnation and in every succeeding version, demands and will demand a fast microprocessor, a big hard disk, a very good display, and lots of RAM. Indeed, don't even consider running Windows on an 80286-based machine, nor on one with less than 4 MB of RAM. You will not be happy.

This issue is particularly important for those who still plan to use a desktop PC at the office, and a notebook or laptop machine on the road. If you use Windows, and a suite of Windows applications, on that desktop machine, you simply must use them on the portable PC, as well. And you have to provide enough *oomph* in that portable to make Windows make sense.

A counter-theory is that, even for those who use Windows at their desks, DOS programs are perfectly satisfactory for lighter-duty use in a road machine.

No, no, no, no.

Once you become accustomed to the Windows style of working—pointing, clicking, graphical displays and the rest of it, and once you become accustomed to Windows applications, you simply won't want to turn back to the anti-matter world of DOS and to a second, separate set of applications.

Try it and you'll go crazy.

And, I guarantee you, try it and you'll scrap the non-Windows setup on your portable itself. And the PC, too, if it isn't powerful enough to support Windows and Windows apps.

A second reason not to oscillate between the world of DOS and DOS applications, and Windows and Windows applications, is that you'll inevitably get trapped by compatibility and file-conversion problems. Most Windows applications will read in data files created by the same vendor's previous non-Windows versions, and sometimes, they'll write, or export, DOS-version-compatible data files back to disk when you're through. But not always—it's too easy to get caught up in programs which handle these translations in only one direction—and file conversions are simply too often unreliable and incomplete to make such a large bet on them.

If you're in the Windows camp, stay in it. At home *and* on the road.

Types of Users, Types of Needs

Just as a taxonomy of the kinds of portable PCs can help you understand the choices available, a typology of portable-PC users can help you by providing several models of portable-PC use, against which you can measure your own needs.

I've picked five distinct types of PC users I've spotted over the years, and matched their needs with the classes of portable computers available today.

If you think you're so unique that there's no one on the planet with needs anything like yours . . . then bully for you. But don't read the following six chapters, because you're about to meet about 95 percent of the portable-PC-using universe, and you may be a little abashed to find yourself in these pages.

An Adjunct to Your Desktop PC . . . Or Your *Only* PC?

In the early days of the portable-PC business—the heyday of the first Compaq and IBM suitcase-sized 25-pound-plus "luggables"—no one thought of portables as second, separate systems, machines they'd use only when they were on the road. Those early suitcases matched the then-current desktop PCs bit for bit when it came to computing power: they were all 4.77 MHz 8088-based machines, usually equipped with the same "huge" 10 MB hard disks we used in desktop computers. And if you wanted something extra—say, a video-display card for an external color monitor, or maybe an internal Hayes modem—it was easy enough to add, since these "portable" behemoths had the same bus-expansion slot design as standard desktop IBM PCs and compatibles: you just plugged in the card and went on your way.

Buying decisions didn't revolve around which portable best complemented the machine on your desk; these *were* the machines on our desks. That we could pack 'em up and haul 'em off to meetings with clients, or home for weekend work, was a bonus, and was what had attracted us to them despite their ungainly size and weight, small display sizes and other compromises—but it was hardly reason enough to buy one as a *second* computer.

But when much smaller, lighter, truly portable PCs began to appear, the idea of buying a portable as a "second computer" began to take hold. Two opposing trends emerged: while portables were getting lighter, smaller and more convenient, but not much more powerful, the power of deskbound machines grew rapidly, and we developed a taste for large monitors, lots of RAM, and hard disks with capacities in the hundreds of megabytes. Thus many came to see portables as *convenience* machines—road warriors, take-homes, workday-extenders—but certainly not as serious replacements for those much more powerful (and much larger and heavier) desktop machines we were coming to think of as our *real* computers.

For a time, it made sense to think of a portable only as an extension of the computing tools already in place on your desk: portables *were* lighter, smaller, and battery-powered . . . but they were also much more feeble computing tools than typical desktop systems.

They had squinchy, hard-to-read LCD displays—and if you plugged an external monitor into a portable's video output connector, you got a coarse, ugly, low-resolution, CGA-level display on that monitor. They had cramped keyboards with a lousy feel and unfortunate, nonstandard compromises on the layout of the keys. They had older, slower microprocessors, running at slower clock speeds, than most desktop computers. They had less RAM than most desktop machines and could accept only limited RAM upgrades—which were often very costly, at a time when prices for standard memory chips were falling sharply. They had very small hard disks—if they had hard disks at all—and those disks were not very fast. They had little or no internal expansion capability—and if they were expandable, they were typically limited to adding an internal modem or required wildly nonstandard devices, usually hooked up through a nonstandard connector to a clumsy, nonstandard external box. They couldn't be connected easily—and often, not at all—to the increasingly ubiquitous local area network in the office. And they were, measured against desktop machines, *very* expensive.

In sum, for several years, while the popularity of laptop, then notebook PCs grew dramatically, they were still not very powerful machines, and certainly not realistic replacements for the desktop machines in general use in business.

But times change. Though few seemed to notice at the time, laptops and notebooks took a quantum leap in *effective* power and convenience in the early 1990s. The appearance of the 386SX generation of notebooks, especially, marked the arrival of a kind of parity between portable and deskbound systems. Though it was and is certainly possible to find desktop PCs more capable than even the hottest notebooks, good notebook PCs came to have about the level of computer firepower found on most desktop systems. Suddenly, it became practical to use just one machine, not two. And in the process, to shed both psychic and financial burdens.

Anyone who's worked with two machines—one kept on the desk in the office, the other kept in an attache case for use on the go—knows what a pain it is to have to reconcile the two systems. The one data file you need absolutely *RIGHT THEN*—and maybe, the one program you need, as well—is always on the other machine. Which leads to that electronic form of absurdist theatre in which the lead character is constantly calling the office and asking someone to FedEx her a disk with the needed file overnight; or to turn on her desktop PC and modem, so she can try to tie into it with a remote-access program; or to print a file from that desktop PC and fax the printout to her; or to any of another half-dozen embarrassing variations.

It gets worse. When she returns from a trip, she has to remember which files on the hard disk in the portable have been changed from the files of the same name that reside on the hard disk in the desktop machine. And transfer those updated files to the Real Computer.

No one needs that kind of hassle. These little notebook-sized boxes are, after all, supposed to make our lives easier and simpler, not more complicated.

They can, they can . . . if we drop outmoded ways of thinking about them. And I think seeing portables only as extensions of the desktop computing environment—not the whole of it—is the place to start that change.

Many of today's notebook PCs are fine replacements for desktop PCs. For some—the minimalists among us, those who try to play a round of golf with two woods and four irons, and can spend a week on the road living out of a traveling bag the size of a cigar box—that means nothing more than plopping the notebook PC down on their desks and going to work. After all, they argue, if you can live with a notebook's display and keyboard on the road, why can't you live with it at your desk?

But if you're accustomed to big, bright, colorful displays and full-size keyboards—and especially, if you rely on constant access to the company's network when you're at work—that's easy, too. Because as part of that revolution in the power and flexibility of notebook PCs in the early 1990s, it became easy to plug those tools into a notebook PC.

Picture this: At your desk you have a Super VGA color monitor, a good keyboard and a mouse—but no computer. When you return from a trip, you pull your notebook out of your brief case and stand it on end, closed, in a little rack near the back of your desk. You plug the keyboard into the notebook's standard external-keyboard jack, the monitor into its standard VGA connector, the mouse into its standard "mouseport" or serial port, and an AC cord into its standard power connector. You plug a Xircom Pocket LAN adapter into the notebook's parallel printer port. If you want access to a local printer as well as to the shared printers on the LAN, you've already attached a Xircom Parallel Port adapter and the cable running to that local printer to that Pocket LAN adapter.

Bang! You're in business. It takes about 12 seconds. *(I just hooked up my notebook at my desk and timed myself: it took me 10.4 seconds. But then, I do this a lot. Should we petition the International Olympic Committee to make this a Summer Games event?)* Some would argue that it's even faster to use a "docking station" system at your desk, with these connections already in place, so all you have to do is slip your notebook into the system when you return. That's good in theory, but I've never seen a really well-thought-out docking system. Compaq and Zenith are getting close, though. (See "Choosing a Docking Station" in *At Your Desk.*)

Now, when you turn on that notebook PC, you have available exactly the same set of tools—programs, data files, hard disk, modem, etc.—that you used on the road. But you also have instant access to the network and all its resources, a keyboard and mouse made for desktop use, a big, color monitor, maybe a laser printer sitting next to your desk.

And when you're ready to go again? It's just as fast to *un*plug those five connectors, slip the notebook PC into your case, and run out the door.

With, you'll note, everything on your travelling computer in exactly the same form and place as on your desktop computer.

Because they're the same machine.

Someday soon, most of that plugging and unplugging will be largely unnecessary. You'll still hook up to an AC power line and to the office network (in a few years, through a cordless connection using radio or light waves), but notebook PCs' built-in color LCD displays will surpass the quality of standard TV-style monitors, and notebook PCs' keyboards will be better, too, complete with built-in mice or trackballs.

But there's no need to wait: today's systems are plenty good enough to make this one-PC approach work well, without compromises. For example, my current notebook PC—a perfectly stock, $2,500 unit from Dell—has built-in Super VGA support through its external video connector that goes all the way to 800 × 600 with 16 colors (and even, uselessly, to 1,024 × 768 with 4 colors). Hardly anyone has noticed how good the built-in video support is in many of today's notebook PCs—but that's to your advantage: you can be the first kid on your block.

If all this sounds a little spacey—*well, sure, I guess you COULD make it work, but why bother?*—then you haven't worked much with a two-PC setup, or you enjoy making life difficult. On the other hand, if this sounds pretty good, but you simply haven't *thought* about it before—well, get to work. And retire that wheezing desktop computer.

The Travelling Executive

One of the easiest types of portable PC users to spot is the travelling executive. I define "executive" broadly here—including everyone from sales people up through senior management at very large companies—because their computing needs and problems are so similar. Indeed, because these requirements are so broadly shared, this is clearly the largest class of portable computer users.

Accordingly, the market has responded to this mainstream user with an amazingly large number of amazingly similar laptop and notebook machines. That's not to say that if you fall into this category, it doesn't much matter which machine you pick, because they're all about the same—*it matters a great deal*—but only that you're in a good position as a mid-market buyer, because there's a rich range of choices, with the attractive prices characteristic of the fat middle of any market.

I define the portable-computer needs of the travelling executive as follows: the machine must be capable of running all the DOS, Windows and *OS/2* applications its owner runs, or would like to run, at his or her desk, and it must run them reasonably quickly, with no serious compromises in performance compared to typical current desktop PCs.

The machine must be battery powered, with a typical real-world three-hour battery life between charges. The battery must be easily user-exchangeable so you can bring along an extra, and it should return to full charge quickly—on the order of an hour's charging time for every hour of working time—not only after, say, a 14-hour charge cycle.

The computer must have an internal hard disk of 40 MB or greater capacity, but it need not have a built-in floppy disk drive, if an external floppy drive is readily and inexpensively available. The display should be reasonably large and bright, and certainly backlit—this user is going to spend long hours at the machine. The keyboard, too, must be decent, with reasonable key-travel distance and touch, standard center-to-center spacing on the keytops, and intelligent placement of cursor, ESCape, and other special keys.

The machine must include, or accept, an internal modem capable of sending data at 2,400 bps or higher, faxes at 9,600 bps or higher. The machine needs to provide support for external monitors, and should deliver at least 800 × 600-pixel × 16-color Super VGA output through a built-in VGA connector. It should have two serial ports, or at least one serial port and a mouse port.

Finally, the machine must be relatively small and light, about 8¹/2 inches deep × 11 inches wide, 1¹/2 to 2 inches thick, weighing less than 8 pounds.

Those are all outer limits, of course; smaller size, lower weight, longer battery life and so on are all welcome, as are intelligent, civilized little touches such as a built-in handle, auto-sensing voltage-switching between 110v and 220v, or a recessed power switch.

If that sounds like I've described any one of maybe a hundred 386SX notebooks available these days, you're close. The differences among those apparently almost-identical machines can be very important, but in general, this class of 386SX notebooks is aimed right at the travelling executive.

Within those broad requirements, of course, there is a great deal of latitude to accommodate personal preferences. You couldn't afford to have someone design a notebook PC just for you—but with the range of today's models, you should be able to find one that works almost as if it *were* designed for you.

For example, I don't think an internal floppy disk drive is necessary, so I look for a machine that trades off a floppy drive for a reduction in weight. And although I want as small a machine as possible, I'm also picky about keyboard size and quality, so I'm not much attracted by machines that do funny things with keytop size, keytop spacing, and key placement, all in the interest of shaving a half-inch off the width of the machine.

I also make frequent computer presentations while I'm travelling, using an external monitor, LCD projection panel or video projector, and so I'm pretty demanding about the quality of external-video support built into a portable I want to call my own. I also like to use a notebook at my desktop, often as my *only* PC at a location; that capability to handle an external monitor when the notebook and I are deskbound counts then, too.

You, however, may constantly exchange data with clients, colleagues, and others while you're on the road, or may find you sleep soundly at night on the road only if you've made a quick-and-dirty backup of the files you've created or changed that day. So a built-in floppy disk drive may be essential for you.

Or you may not care so much about keyboard quality—if you're not inputting much data, keyboard quality clearly becomes much less important—and thus are willing to sacrifice keyboard "feel" in favor of getting the smallest machine possible. Or you may think PC-based presentations are for the birds, and never plan to use your notebook PC at your desk, so built-in support for external video would be a nonissue for you.

The point is simple: Travelling executives should demand a capable machine, one that can function as an extension of their offices. Saddling them with a note-taking-level portable, or burdening them with the size and weight of a power-portable that could double as a network server-cum-missile launcher, is foolish.

If this little profile sounds familiar—if you think I'm talking about you—look for a machine in the middle of the notebook/laptop market, and exploit that proliferation of 386SX boxes available today by demanding one that caters to your taste and your idiosyncrasies.

A final tip: In my experience, a significant number of travelling executives at first underestimate how much they'll use a notebook PC, how useful and important it will become to them. Thus they tend to underbuy—choosing, for example, to save money by buying backwards a generation in notebooks, getting a 12 MHz 80286 machine with a small 20 MB hard disk, or maybe even a really low-end 8088/8086 floppy-only notebook. If, after all, they're only going to use it as a note-taker, and maybe to stay in touch via electronic mail, they reason, why do they need more?

If over time those do turn out to be their primary uses of the machine, then that was a good decision, and a reasonable compromise. Certainly the sub-$1,000 price of these note-taking-level machines appeals, and if you buy the right one, you can save weight and space, as well.

But much more often than not, the error is in buying too little computer, not too much. If you're the CEO and buy the wrong machine, it's easy to get rid of it and get another overnight. If you're the regional manager, it may be fairly easy for you, too. But if you're a mid-level manager who has to account for the funds you spend and live with what you've asked Purchasing to buy for you, then swapping your underpowered notebook for the right kind of machine may be difficult or impossible.

I don't want to strain your budget (or your back) with more computer than you'll need, but before you decide your needs are really a notch down from those set out in this chapter, think carefully about how your work habits have changed over time, how your responsibilities have grown . . . and how tough it would be to get out of a bad buying decision.

For Power Users Only

Tell me about the PC on your desk now. Is it an 80486-based machine—maybe even an early 80586? Is its hard disk one of those hundreds-of-megabytes jobs? Does it have a big monitor—17 inches, or maybe even larger? Running at 1,024 x 768 pixels . . . or even 1,280 x 1,024? Does it have 8 MB, 12 MB, or even more RAM? Do you have a CD-ROM drive connected? A scanner? A second, external hard disk? Two or more modems?

Does the nameplate on the front read "Cray"—or maybe, "Caterpillar"?

And tell me about the work you do: CAD? Desktop publishing? Elaborate presentations? Complicated business graphics?

If the answers to a lot of those questions are *Yes,* then you're a candidate for a true blockbuster notebook or laptop. Indeed, you'll probably gravitate towards a laptop as you search for a machine, since you won't find a notebook stout enough to meet your needs. The machine you'll settle on will be bigger, heavier, and clumsier than the portable PCs most of us use, and it almost certainly won't run on batteries, limiting your definition of "portable" to "somewhere near an AC outlet." But if it's what you need to do your job, then by definition it's the right choice—and worth its substantial cost, size and weight.

In sum, if you're a real power-user, you probably already know that. After all, you've had a lot of experience upgrading and trading-out your PCs for something more powerful every six months for the last few years . . . .

But in my experience, very few PC users really need these ultra-powerful portables. Even if you do have a muscle-box on your desk now, consider whether you really need to take all that functionality out in the field. Is your portable machine perhaps going to be used, instead, for more typical office-productivity applications—word-processing, spreadsheets, databases, communications—most of the time, and only as a kind of show-and-tell box for things such as CAD and business graphics? In other words, to show others what you've created at your desk?

If so, do you really want to hobble yourself with the size, weight, and price penalties of a power portable when the great majority of the time you don't need all that power?

All this said, I do know a few people who are absolutely justified in using high-end, high-power laptops. One, a consulting engineer, does extremely complex hydro-system planning. He downloads huge models constructed in his office on a 50 MHz 80486 power-PC to his DolchPak lunchbox-shaped portable, then takes that out with him into the boondocks. His portable even has a good-looking color display (which added about three grand to its price), because color is used as a critical differentiator in his models. At job sites, he wows the other engineers and—*more importantly*—the clients by booting up the Dolch, loading a model, then playing what-if with the graphics in the model as his clients ask him questions.

Because he can usually satisfy their urge to look at alternative solutions right there in the field, he comes back to his office with the job finished or nearly so, dramatically reducing the number of site-visits and client meetings. His clients think of him as a kind of computer god; he knows it's all in the Dolch.

Another acquaintance, an architect, does something similar to that with a Compaq 486 color portable. He uses AutoCAD and AutoShade to produce 3-D views of parts of projects, then takes this big, heavy machine out to clients' offices to give them a little show-and-tell routine. They eat it up: they feel part of the process, and they think he's right on top of the job. As a matter of fact, he *is* on top of the job . . . but not necessarily because he puts on that good show.

Finally, I know a CPA with a mid-sized regional accounting firm who has a 486-laptop based local-area network he carries to clients' office for audits. He sets up a system using this 486 laptop as a mini-server in an unused conference room in the client's office, runs Ethernet cables around the room to 386SX laptops and notebooks he sets up for each CPA on the audit team to use, and in about 30 minutes he has a miniature replica of the system in their own office. Because the setup uses the same software they use in the office, there's nothing new for his CPAs and para-professionals to learn. Because they have all the tools they need to complete the audit right there on the job, no one has to make compromises on the tests they're performing on the client's books. And because it's a mini-network, everyone in the room can tap into the same pool of common data built up over the few days or weeks of this on-site audit. (The room, incidentally, is a mess: it looks like a motel room occupied by a bunch of techno-nerd college students on Spring Break. Network cables run down the table, drape over the backs of chairs, and so on. But the firm's clients love it: it's clear *their* accountants are on top of this computer stuff. That it also saves clients money, by allowing the CPAs to complete their audit in less time, doesn't escape clients' notice, either.)

None of these, of course, is a typical portable-computer application—which is exactly my point.

If you really do have special needs which demand a super-powerful portable PC, then by all means spend $10,000 or more for one of these heavy, clumsy beasts. But if your needs are more modest, lower your sights. You'll save money and dislocated shoulders in the process.

Notetakers

If 386SX, 386SL, and 486SX notebooks represent the broad middle of the market, and muscle-box 80486DXs and even, soon enough, 80586s represent the high end, what's the one-step-down class of machines that must be right for the occasional portable-PC user? Clearly, it's the flock of now remarkably inexpensive 80286 machines that fills the shelves and ads of discounters and close-out specialists.

Let me tell you, my friends: some of these are sweet machines, indeed.

The all-time champs among this now-extinct breed are the Sharp 6220PC, the Texas Instruments TravelMate 2000, and the CompuAdd Companion 2000. It's a three-way tie, because all three are really the same machine: though designed by Sharp in Japan, Texas Instruments made them all, on an assembly line in Texas. The only variations in the three have to do with slightly different built-in features in the system BIOS chip, very minor external-design differences, the choice of bundled software, and, of course, the documentation, prepared separately by each of the three companies.

These machines—for brevity's sake I'll call them all TI 2000s—had a brief moment in the sun, in mid-to-late 1990, when their features, human factors, and price put them way ahead of the competition. The TI 2000 even won PC Magazine's vaunted Technical Excellence Award at the Fall 1990 COMDEX trade show. But the tidal wave of 386SX machines was just about to break on the shores of the U.S., and that glut of 386SXs meant that by mid-1991, prices on these three machines were tumbling from an original list price of over $3,000 (and a street price of about $2,795) to a final level of about $795 at the lowest-price close-out firms.

Gone but hardly forgotten, you can often still find them—especially the Texas Instruments version, which apparently stayed in production longer than the other two marques—new in the box, in close-out centers.

Outclassed in power and features by the 386SX-generation machines, and (like every other 286 PC) unable to run Windows with anything like acceptable performance, these machines—and all their 286-notebook brethren, even at today's bargain-basement prices, no longer represent good buys for most business-PC users.

But if your needs are less on the general-business computing level, and more on the note-taking level, they can be a superb choice. Buy one and I can guarantee you that sooner or later you're going to trade up to a more powerful machine; and you may as well accept now that a notebook PC you bought for under $1,000 new is not going to have much resale value.

But if your computing needs are light, these gems can be an incredibly cost-effective choice.

What's so hot about the TI 2000 and its look-alike relatives from CompuAdd and Sharp? First, they're uncommonly small and light, at about $8^1/2 \times 11 \times 1^1/2$ inches thick, and less than $4^1/2$ pounds. That's thinner and lighter than practically any 386SX machine, and half the weight of some of them. It even matches the size and weight of some early "subnotebooks." Yet that slender box holds 1 MB of RAM (upgradeable to only 3 MB), a 20 MB hard disk, a good keyboard, and a huge (10-inch diagonal), sharp, bright, backlit display that still outclasses most notebook PCs' screens.

The internal battery gives you two to two-and-a-half hours of use; it takes a few seconds to change, but at least it is user-exchangeable . . . and extra batteries are still available from most dealers closing out these machines. If you don't mind a little extra size and weight, a separate, clip-on battery "slice" which attaches to the back of the machine will give you five hours or more of working time without changing batteries. Both battery systems recharge on the ideal 1:1 basis—that is, one hour of charging time for each hour of battery life.

There's no internal 3 1/2-inch floppy-disk drive, but an external drive is (or was) available at low cost. A 2,400 bps internal voice/fax modem is available, too, and works well. There are also external numeric keypads, desktop docking stations, external video-output connectors and other accessories—but this is a grab-it-and-go machine, for which such big-system extensions make little sense. If you need those add-ons, you probably shouldn't buy a TI 2000 in the first place.

If you want a notebook PC for taking notes away from the office, for some word processing on the road, handling the occasional 1-2-3 worksheet, and staying in touch by e-mail and fax when you're travelling, these are the machines for you.

And though I've talked here about only the Sharp/Texas Instruments/CompuAdd machines, many of their 80286 siblings could work well for you, too—though with some weight, size and performance compromises.

However—and this is a big however—there is one serious drawback to these note-takers for some users.

If you use Windows on your desktop PC, or if you think you *will* be using Windows in the near future, stay away from 286 machines, period. Despite manufacturers' claims, they don't run Windows well at all; performance slows to a crawl. You'll also miss out on running Windows in its 386 Enhanced mode, which is where it shines; that only works on 386SX, 386DX, and higher machines. Finally, once you get used to working Windows-style on your desktop, and get used to using Windows applications, you don't want to have to learn and use a second, different set of programs on the road.

That way lies madness. Don't do it.

No doubt I've just irritated some readers who already own 286 notebooks and use them every day for a broad range of computing tasks.

Please don't be insulted: I know they're good machines, because I still use one myself. A lot. When I'm off on a trip and want only to work on a column or two and stay in touch via electronic mail, I grab my trusty TI 2000. Bigger, heavier, and more capable PCs be damned: I want light and small, period. (I also love the big bright displays on these machines, which sadly and puzzlingly, have not migrated up to more recent models.)

If you're among those daily users of 286 notebooks, and you think I'm a heel for damning them with this faint praise, think about it for a minute; would you buy the same machine again today, if you were going out for a brand-new portable? I didn't think so.

Travelling Presenters

Strict application of the typology set up in this section would disallow another category called "travelling presenters." After all, as I'll admit in a second, these people, who frequently run computerized slide shows from their portable PCs—sometimes showing the material on the screen of the PC itself, for an audience of just two or three, but much more often presenting the material with the assistance of a video projector, LCD projection plate or just a large monitor—are certainly travelling executives, and are also very often power users.

But it's just that crossover—the intersection of the needs of the travelling executive and the power user—that leads me to carve out another category for Travelling Presenters. Just as their use of a portable PC is out of the mainstream (though perhaps not for much longer), their needs also deserve special attention.

Not long ago, it wasn't realistic to think about taking your PC-based show on the road in a notebook PC. Notebooks just didn't have enough power and flexibility; you had to move up to a full-fledged laptop machine—and even then, one of the larger, heavier, higher-priced models. Toshiba's 386-based T5200 was a popular choice, as was Toshiba's T3200SXC, which has less computer firepower, but dazzled us with its bright, sharp, colorful, built-in active-matrix color LCD display.

Today, presenters who can be sure they'll always be showing their material via an external system—feeding a video signal through the PC's external-video port to a large monitor, or to a video projector or LCD projection plate—can often get by just fine with a high-end notebook PC. With sufficient memory (typically 4 MB or more; 8 to 10 MB is better), a sizeable, fast-access hard disk and good built-in external-video support, today's better notebooks are perfectly capable of handling the demands of a typical PC-based presentation, presented on an external display system.

Two caveats, one of which you heard coming in that last sentence: First, today's notebook PCs are generally NOT up to the demands of presenting shows on their built-in displays. This will change, to some degree, soon, as higher-quality active-matrix thin-film transistor color-LCD displays begin to appear in high-end notebook PCs. But even then, the screen size will limit you to showing your materials to just one or two other people—with all of you hunched uncomfortably over your notebook.

The second caveat has to do with the definition of a "typical PC-based presentation." Today, that means static screens like 35mm slides, displayed one after another. There may be some nifty visual effects from slide to slide—a new slide wipes away the previous one, or the first disappears in a cloud of sparkles as the second appears, or the next slide zooms up to full-screen size atop the old one—but these are still static images.

As the new PC multimedia products mature, it will be possible to include high-quality sound, animated images, much more sophisticated wipes and dissolves, user-interactivity, control of external full-motion video (from a VCR or laser disk, and maybe from a CD-ROM disk), and maybe even nearly full-motion video entirely from within the PC. These shows are unlikely candidates for even the most powerful notebook PCs for a long time to come, because of their demand for system resources. They'll take a lot of RAM, a very large hard disk, special controller cards for external devices, and a level of audio playback not even approached by today's best notebook PC sound systems.

You can certainly "play" these presentations from a high-powered laptop now: 80486 SX and DX laptop PCs from Toshiba and Compaq already deliver the power and flexibility required for the job. But those presentations will still require an external display medium, external sound-playback facilities, and external drives for CD-ROMs, video cassettes, laser discs, and so on.

So if you're bitten by the multimedia bug, and want to take your act on the road, consider carefully just how much raw computing power you need in your next portable. Almost no matter your guess, you'll aim too low.

Off to College

The last type of portable PC user in my categories is the student heading off to college. Businesspeople may wonder why, in a book about increasing business productivity, I address the needs of college students. I do so because I get a constant stream of letters from parents—businesspeople all, PC users to the core—asking what kind of computer I think they should send off to State U. with Junior in the Fall.

It's a good question, with a constantly changing answer. Not so long ago, PCs were so expensive that the best answer was "whatever you can buy used, at a reasonable price," or "whatever you have on your desk at home now; then buy a new PC for yourself." But the emergence of full-powered notebook PCs and the growing role of computers in modern life suggest that your scholar deserves better. Of course, plummeting computer prices don't hurt, either; Mom and Dad are more likely to be able to afford decent machines for their college-bound kids now than a few years ago.

If ever there was a situation made for portable PCs—and the smaller the better—it's in the hands of a college student. Whether in a dorm, frat house, or apartment—does anyone live in boarding houses at college anymore, as I did long ago?—a notebook PC, or even a sub-notebook-sized machine, is a perfect fit with students' space, needs, and temperament.

If you need a machine for your student, I'd suggest you look at a few of the lower-cost machines in the full-fledged Travelling Executives category. A simpler, less expensive note-taking-level machine may at first appeal, but remember that you want this machine to last four years (you hope!), and in just a couple of years—if not tomorrow!—your student's computing needs are likely to far outstrip a simple note-taker. For that reason I also have some reservations about the sub-notebooks, although full-featured "subs" might fit the bill.

What I really want to do here is steer parents away from that very advice I once gave so freely: clean off the desk in the corner of the den by sending off to college with your son or daughter whatever you've been using as a home PC. Those often-obsolete machines lurking in the corners of our dens, playrooms, bedrooms, and basement offices just aren't up to the needs of college students today.

Spring for the two grand or so it will cost to give your kid a decent notebook PC and a simple printer. It will be money well spent.

Buying Smart: Notebooks for the '90s

Buying decisions for notebook and laptop PCs are often as much emotional as they are technological and practical. A friend once described his brand-new, sleek, four-pound, matte-black NEC Ultralite as "four pounds of raw sex appeal"—and I knew immediately what he was talking about.

The rational among us make buying decisions based on carefully considered analyses of the various components of a computer, matched to a sober assessment of our needs—and our budgets. Or at least we like to think we do.

For the confirmed rationalists—and also for those of us who try to act like them at cocktail parties and in budget-review meetings—here's everything you'll need to know to make a wise choice in a portable PC.

Processor Power

I'm on slightly shaky ground here. In an industry which makes its hottest products obsolete every 18 months or so, it's a dangerous thing for anyone writing a book to say that at this moment, the microprocessor of choice for a notebook PC is the 80386SX. Pick up this book a year or two from now and that might be out of date; the 80486SX, or even a later chip, may be King of the Hill in the notebook world.

But the history and unique position of the 386SX generation of notebooks is interesting and instructive.

Yes, right now the Intel 80386SX chip *is* the one that's driving the notebook-PC business. But this isn't only an evolutionary step; the 386SX marked a watershed in the evolution of personal computers. Along with its later sister chip, Intel's 386SL, and similar "clone" chips from Advanced Micro Devices, Cyrix, and others, the "SX" made it possible for the first time to produce something like an uncompromised battery-powered, fits-in-your-attache-case computer. The compatibility of the 386SX with the dominant 80386 instruction set meant that computers using the SX could run essentially any program you could run on a desktop PC. And while the performance of the 386SX series chips certainly wasn't quite up to the level of that found in Intel's full-fledged 80386 (properly, the 80386DX), nor in the later 80486 family, it isn't bad.

Yes, you can detect a difference in the execution speed of programs running on 386SX computers, versus that same code running on 386DXs and 486s, but it isn't that big a difference, and it just doesn't matter that much.

In fact, the best evidence of that satisfactory 386SX level of performance isn't found in the portable-PC world at all, but in how quickly SX-based desktop PCs became the standard in business. Almost overnight they conquered the 80286 generation; yet 386SXs are generally powerful enough that corporate computing managers didn't think the extra *oomph* from moving up to a 80386DX, or even to an 80486, was worth the extra dough.

Intel and the 80386SX chip were also lucky, in a sense, because shortly after the chip appeared, other important computer-system improvements began to arrive and were quickly absorbed into that delicate balancing act of designing a notebook PC. Triple-twist nematic LCD screens became available. Backlit screens began to make sense. Miniature hard disks with 20–60 MB capacity materialized. Nickel-hydride batteries appeared, extending the time between charges for portables by about a third.

As these advances were consolidated into what became a flood of remarkably similar 386SX-based notebook PCs, the chip itself in effect began to get the credit for a whole range of technological advances it hadn't really had much to do with.

And the coalescing of all those technologies into the 386SX generation of notebook PCs delivered a product we'd never seen before: a six-to-seven pound portable computer with a readable screen, a built-in hard disk, battery life of two to three hours, computing speed comparable to many current desktop computers, and a reasonable price.

Thus the 386SX generation of notebooks PCs became an important hinge-point: buy a computer with a lesser microprocessor (such as Intel's 80286, or 8086 or 8088, or their NEC and AMD clones) and you know you're making serious compromises; buy a computer with a more powerful microprocessor (the 80486SX or DX, for example) and you'd better have had a good reason for that decision, or you paid a substantial premium for nothing—and, probably, also paid a penalty in terms of size, weight, battery power, and other important features.

As new, 3.3-volt low-voltage variations on the 386SX design, such as Intel's own 386SL, appear (providing even longer effective battery life), and as the aggressive pricing of faster 386SX clones from AMD pushes performance up at the same time prices fall even lower (one of the sweetest rewards of the computer industry; if only Detroit worked that way), the SX-generation notebooks are likely to hold their position as the price-and-value champs in portable computing for some time. Machines built with the Intel 486SX will elbow into this market, but in truth, they are (just like the 486DXs versus 386DXs) really just gussied-up 386SXs. The fundamental equation is unlikely to change for a while.

The issue of just who should buy more- and less-powerful notebook PCs, respectively, than 386SXs is addressed in *Types of Users, Types of Needs.* Certainly there are good reasons, set out there, for some, for buying up or down from that 386SX hinge-point. But only if you're *sure* you fit into one of the "other" categories.

For now, for most of us, the right answer is usually a 386SX-family answer.

Memory

There's long been one easy answer to the question *"How much memory should I install in my PC?"*—as much as you can afford. And for some notebook and laptop PC users, that's still pretty good advice. You can almost always wring better performance out of a PC by adding more memory.

But there are limits, and it's foolish to stretch memory beyond what you can realistically use. In addition, notebook and laptop PC users pay a hidden penalty for lots of RAM: because the dynamic random-access memory (DRAM) we use in PCs must be constantly refreshed, it exerts a constant, if very low-level, draw on the system power supply. So the more memory you have, the greater the battery drain and the shorter the running time between charges.

On the other hand, plenty of memory in a portable means you can actually *save* battery life in another way, through caching frequently used data on the hard disk in a block of RAM set aside for that purpose. The current drawn by the hard disk in a portable PC, as it repeatedly searches for, reads, and transfers data from the hard disk into memory, is second only to the power drawn to backlight the display in depleting the batteries. Thus, the less you use the hard disk, the longer your batteries can power the machine between fill-ups. So creating a large RAM cache, which can reduce hard-disk access by as much as 75–80 percent under some circumstances, can make an important difference in battery life.

You can also use extra RAM to create a virtual disk in memory—a "RAM disk"—to which you can copy, before you begin work, programs that make repeated trips to the hard disk not for data, but for program overlays. Large programs use this technique extensively, swapping portions of their code in and out of memory; with them, a RAM disk can not only save battery power when you're running these programs, it can also speed up the execution of these programs very significantly.

The moral: Don't install more memory than you really need . . . but strike a balance among the competing factors here: the machine's inherent RAM capacity, the cost of RAM chips or SIMMs, frequency of hard-disk accesses, and battery life.

My rules of thumb for several different portable-PC configurations:

Recommended Memory Configurations

System	Minimum	Better	Optimum
Laptop PC, any CPU, DOS	1 MB	2 MB	2 MB
Laptop PC, any CPU, Windows	4 MB	8 MB	12 MB
Notebook PC, 286, DOS	1 MB	2 MB	2 MB
Notebook PC, 286, Windows	NR	NR	NR
Notebook PC, 386SX, DOS	1 MB	2 MB	4 MB
Notebook PC, 386SX, Windows	4 MB	6 MB	8 MB
Notebook PC, 386SL, DOS	1 MB	2 MB	4 MB
Notebook PC, 386SL, Windows	5 MB	8 MB	12 MB
Notebook PC, 486SX/DX, DOS	2 MB	4 MB	4 MB
Notebook PC, 486SX/DX, Windows	8 MB	12 MB	16 MB

NR = configuration not recommended

These are, remember, only recommendations. They're based on the assumptions that you'll create and use a large disk-cache, using a program such as SMARTDRV or Super PC-Kwik (see "Disk Caching" in "A Notebook PC Software Kit," later in this section), and perhaps a RAM disk as well, in a DOS-only environment; and that you'll want a cache in Windows, plus plenty of memory for multiple Windows applications open at once.

Buying more RAM is usually one of the cheapest performance boosts you can give a notebook or laptop PC. And over time, as you use more and larger programs and find additional uses for "extra" RAM, it's an investment you'll never regret.

Hard Disks

Though there were a couple of notable early laptop PCs without hard disks, they soon faded. Toshiba's T1000 won attention as the lightest and smallest laptop of its time by using only a single 3½-inch floppy drive and an optional-but-essential built-in RAM drive; and NEC's first UltraLite won fame, if few customers, with its 1 MB or 2 MB "silicon hard disks," plus a slot for mounting nonvolatile memory cards which came preloaded with software. (Both machines, interestingly, would be called notebook PCs today; but both appeared in the late 1980s, before that term came into use.)

These were clever machines, but the lack of a reasonable means of mass storage killed them both. PC users need hard disks, and machines without them are so severely compromised that they are soon set aside. You may be able to get along with only a relatively small 20 MB hard disk—about the smallest-capacity drive we've seen installed in laptop and notebook PCs so far—or your needs may reach up to the 100 MB-and-beyond level of today's top-of-the-line notebooks, or even into the much larger disks installed in the remaining laptops.

But whatever size hard disk you choose, make sure it's big enough to make your portable PC really useful.

Once again, here are some guidelines, based on the power of the machine and your preference for DOS or Windows, for choosing the right-size hard disk:

Recommended Hard Disk Sizes

System	Minimum	Better	Optimum
Laptop PC, DOS	40 MB	60 MB	80 MB
Laptop PC, any CPU, Windows	80 MB	150 MB	300 MB
Notebook PC, 286, DOS	20 MB	40 MB	60 MB
Notebook PC, 286, Windows	NR	NR	NR
Notebook PC, 386SX/SL, DOS	40 MB	60 MB	80 MB
Notebook PC, 386SX/SL, Windows	80 MB	120 MB	200 MB
Notebook PC, 486SX/DX, DOS	80 MB	120 MB	200 MB
Notebook PC, 486SX/DX, Windows	120 MB	150 MB	200 MB

NR = configuration not recommended

Few PC users believe they have a hard disk that's too large. Additional increments of hard-disk capacity cost proportionally much less than the first 40 to 60 MB of capacity, yet give you plenty of room to grow. Windows users, especially, can always use more hard disk space, for such system enhancements as a permanent swapfile, and for fonts, additional programs and all those silly geegaws we stuff into our Windows machines.

Upgrading later is costly, because it means tossing out that drive you bought when you bought the notebook or laptop originally: these machines have space inside for only one hard disk. Make the jump now to a hard disk of sufficient capacity to see you through the probable useful life of the machine.

Displays

Some people think of a computer's keyboard as its primary user interface. I disagree; that title belongs to displays. If you can't *see* what you're doing, no keyboard in the world is going to help. So I find myself casting an unusually critical eye on laptop and notebook PCs' displays, looking for something that will be as easy to see—or better, even *easier* to see—than the best desktop-PC displays.

The good news: they're not that far apart.

Anyone who's used portable computers over the years has put up with a lot of sorry displays. Most of the LCD screens shipped with small computers since the first laptops appeared a half-dozen years ago have fallen beneath any reasonable threshold of viewing ease and comfort; some have been simply beneath contempt, period.

Today's monochrome LCD displays fall, broadly, into two categories: backlit and reflective. The former, in the clear majority on today's machines, typically use some form of cold cathode backlighting to make the display easier to see. Not only are onscreen characters easy to see; you can also work in little or no light. That's an important advantage for, say, the frequent flyer, who may want to work long after the rest of the folks in the cabin have nodded off. Sure, you can keep the little eyeball-spotlight in the overhead turned on, but you'll get some angry stares. Worse, that overhead light never falls where you really need it, anyway.

Backlit screens do have one major disadvantage: they can be very hard to read, perversely, in bright light. Take the typical state-of-the-art backlit machine outdoors on a decent day, and the display that looked so good in the dim light indoors will wash out in the bright light of day. On some machines, turning down the backlighting makes sense; the inherent reflectivity of the LCD then delivers an OK image. But most backlit displays were clearly designed to be used in moderate to very low light-level settings.

The reflective type of LCD displays shines—literally—in bright light. As sorry as reflective LCD panels can be in low light, they come into their own in decent-to-good light. Indeed, because I fairly often take a PC outdoors on a pretty day to work under a tree, or at the lake or beach, I keep an old (and now otherwise largely valueless) reflective-display laptop PC around for just those occasions. (Those are also not the most congenial working environments for portable computers, so I also see the machine as cheap insurance against, say, getting sand into the hard-disk drive of my "real" notebook PC.)

Reflective displays have another saving grace: they take much less power than backlit screens. But if you can't see the screen on your notebook PC, what does it matter if its batteries are fully charged and ready to run the thing?

Except for very special circumstances—subnotebook PCs, for example, where size and battery-life considerations force us into using reflective displays—I think the days of reflective LCD screens on portable computers are over. Look for a big, bright, backlit display when you go portable-PC shopping.

Of course, the notion of "big" is subjective, but for many of us, screen size is almost as important as screen brightness and clarity. I love big displays, such as the 10-inch-diagonal backlit screen found on the Sharp 6220 and its look-alikes, described in "Notetakers" earlier in this book. Unfortunately, few 386-level notebook PCs have appeared with screens to match those discontinued Sharp 286s. But recent models do offer hope: some are coming close to the Sharp's screen size.

Watch out for a vendor trying to palm off on you a display built to one of the older screen-resolution standards. The IBM Video Graphics Array standard—640 × 480 pixels—reigns supreme today, and you want nothing less. Tandy, Toshiba and a few others tried to keep alive two of the early, awful LCD-display compromises—the infamous CGA, and nearly-infamous "double-dot CGA" levels—long after their time had passed.

Again: VGA, and nothing less.

Watch out, too, for the proportions of the display. Some displays squeeze the image vertically, with the result that if you show a pie chart onscreen, you see something that looks more like an egg chart. This may not be critically important if you don't plan to run graphics programs on the machine—but even your text displays will be somewhat distorted.

What about color?

Color displays change the rules in laptop and notebook PCs pretty dramatically. If you're sure you want color—if you even *think* you want color—keep reading: the next chapter, "Do You Really *Need* Color?," addresses those issues.

Do You Really *Need* Color?

Those used to using color monitors on their desktop PCs—which means about 90 percent-plus of all business-PC users today, according to my personal and highly unscientific survey—sometimes think they have to have a color display on their portable PCs as well. It's logical, it's nice, and it's expensive. It also introduces some compromises you may not like.

There are two types of color portable-computer displays: passive-matrix LCDs, which offer so-so color, contrast, and brightness, can be powered by batteries, and are reasonably priced; and active-matrix LCDs, which produce great color, superb contrast and brightness, have an appetite for power that can normally be met only by an AC outlet, and carry prices many of us just won't (or can't) pay.

There is no middle ground here, and I don't expect to see one emerge. I do expect to see passive-matrix designs get somewhat better—but not nearly as good as the best active-matrix designs. And I expect to see both the price for active-matrix panels fall and their power requirements decline, as well—but not, in either case, to the levels of today's passive-matrix systems.

So it's a classic computer conundrum: do you want pretty good quality and a good price, or great quality and a much higher price?

Of course all of this begs the issue of whether you really *want* color, which is what this chapter is all about. But price is an important part of this decision, so let's get it out of the way. You can buy a good 386SL notebook PC today with a 32- or 64-step gray-scale monochrome LCD display for about $2,500. Choose a passive-matrix color display and that price—same PC—goes up to about $3,500. Choose an active-matrix color display and that same PC costs maybe $2,000 more, or about $5,500—twice as much as the same machine with a monochrome display, at least half again as much as with a passive-matrix color display.

Hmmm, did I hear you changing your mind? Is "wanting" color really the issue here, not "needing" it . . . ?

I look at the Color Conundrum this way: if you're going to use your PC for Windows and Windows applications, spend the extra money and get the active-matrix color unit. Windows and Windows apps use color on the intuitive level, not merely as decoration. That is, subtle use of onscreen color-coding actually helps you *use* the program.

If you're convinced you're not going to be a Windows user, save the money: you'll be happy with the cheaper, brighter, higher-contrast monochrome display.

And if you plan to use your PC for travelling presentations, where you're showing a PC slide show to someone else on the machine's built-in display, by all means go all the way for the active-matrix unit. It's worth the difference.

Just make sure you have deep pockets, and work close to an AC outlet.

Modems: Built-in or External?

First, let's get this straight: *you want a modem for your portable PC.* Forfeiting the ability to communicate through your notebook or laptop computer throws away a good deal of its value. Even if you're not presently a modem user—no electronic mail, no CompuServe, no online data searches, no remote links to the office's computers—*get a modem.* It will quickly become an integral part of your portable-computing workstyle.

That out of the way, do you want an internal or external modem?

I've changed my mind 180 degrees on this. Or maybe, 179 degrees. I once thought external modems were loopy, a foolish idea for dorky people who didn't think through their use of a portable computer. Perfectly satisfactory internal modems were available—*are* available—for almost all the interesting laptop and notebook PCs. Some notebooks even come with internal modems already installed.

And an internal modem is the ultimate in convenience: you can't lose it or leave it behind. You can't misplace its transformer, power cord, or serial cable—because it doesn't have any of those things. Just plug a wire from the modem into a nearby telephone jack, fire-up your communications software, and go to work. Built-in modems typically run at 2,400 bps, about as fast as most of us need to communicate at this point by computer, and many are available with fax-sending capabilities, too.

So, I thought, who'd want to mess with an external modem?

Then I started fooling around with Telebit QBlazer. This external modem is a tiny cube, about 2 1/2 inches on each side, weighing just a few ounces. It has an internal nine-volt battery (which runs down pretty quickly . . .), so no external power supply transformer and cords are necessary. A simple, short cable runs from the QBlazer to a serial port on my notebook PC, and the usual wire runs from the QBlazer to a telephone jack in the wall. That's it. Nice gizmo.

Still, it's an *external* modem, one more thing to bring along, one more thing to use. Why put up with that?

Because the QBlazer gives me *38,400* bps.

I said just a minute ago that 2,400 bps was about as fast as most of us need to communicate today, and that's true. For checking e-mail, sending the occasional file to a colleague, and other routine, fairly low-level uses of PC communications, 2,400 bps performance is fine.

But more and more lately, I've been shipping big files back and forth to my office and to clients. And more and more, I've been logging onto the PC on my desk from afar, running Windows remotely. And for those jobs, 2,400 bps is, approximately speaking, hopeless.

So I turned to the QBlazer. And was floored by how fast 38,400 bps really is.

There is some trickery afoot here, and we really shouldn't call the QBlazer, or any of the other so-called 38,400 bps modems available "38,400 bps" systems. They really run at 9,600 bps and use data-compression technology to squeeze the fat out of your file before sending it, then unsqueeze that fat right back into it at the receiving end. The net effective transmission speed, after the file is decompressed by the receiving PC, is as much as 38,400 bps. Of course, you need an identical, or compatible, modem at the other end of the connection to get this kind of performance; otherwise, the connection drops to the fastest speed supported by the *slower* of the two modems.

Or even lower, if phone-line noise is a problem.

But who cares if the QBlazer and the others in its class use smart electronics to deliver an effective high rate of throughput? When I'm sitting on the side of the bed in the Four Seasons Somewhere, I'm interested in how *long* it takes to get the job done, not *how* it gets done.

Especially if the data gets there correctly. Which is the other advantage of the QBlazer—though to be fair, an advantage shared these days by many modems, including those that run at much slower effective speeds. Any modem you want to use today uses a variation on the Microcom Networking Protocol, almost always abbreviated as "MNP," to do real-time error-checking during transmissions. The combination of error checking and file compression available under the various levels of MNP implementation means you get both very high effective transfer speeds and also guaranteed-accurate communications.

So what do I do?

I cheat: I use both an internal 2,400 bps MNP5 fax/data modem, and also, sometimes, the external QBlazer modem. If I'm just going to log onto a service such as MCI Mail, a third-party electronic-mail provider, to check for messages, I use the built-in modem. Since many of these services can be accessed only through gateway PADs ("packet assembler-disassemblers") around the country—which won't work faster than 2,400 bps—I lose nothing. In any case, e-mail doesn't require higher speed.

Then, when I sit down to run a long file-transfer session to a client's PC, or to log onto my desktop PC, running Windows, remotely, I plug in the QBlazer. I use a second QBlazer at my desk as my normal modem, so there's no problem with compatibility in these high-speed connections.

We're going to see a lot of tiny, high-speed modems like the QBlazer emerge over the next few years. Many will be good, and many of us who consider ourselves power users will succumb to their high-performance allure, preferring them over the convenience of slower, built-in units. At some point, of course, even built-in modems will offer this kind of performance, and then I'll probably retire my road-weary QBlazer.

What's right for you? Almost certainly, a built-in 2,400 bps voice/fax modem. Unless, of course, you like to see that data in the huge files you're sending someone on the other side of the country absolutely roar by on your notebook's screen. Or unless you want to run Windows. Or unless you just want the fastest and neatest tool.

I can't be a hypocrite here: I succumbed. With the penalty that I now carry the QBlazer when I travel. Along with a notebook with a built-in modem.

Hey, look: I never said I was perfect.

Do You Really Want a Floppy Drive?

This one's almost theological, I'm afraid. I've been in long, loud arguments with my friends at computer magazines about this; the group always splits immediately into the pros and the cons on this—and there's always a lot more heat than light to our arguments.

So I'm going to make my case for *not* buying a notebook PC with a built-in floppy drive. If you agree with me, great; if not—well, you're still in pretty good company.

Proposed: Notebook PCs don't really need floppy drives. They add a surprising amount of bulk and a not inconsiderable amount of weight, thereby needlessly increasing your load, making the machine thicker and heavier than it needs to be.

Since I prefer a smaller, lighter machine over the largely theoretical advantages of having a floppy disk with me on the road, I'll always go for the floppyless machine.

Why no floppy drive? Well, what do you do with it?

- ***You use it to load new software.*** You usually do that at your desk anyway, right?
- ***You use it to copy files from your notebook PC's hard disk to a floppy, to give that floppy to a friend or colleague.*** But how often do you really do that when you're away from the office?

- ***You use it to make backups.*** But friends, I am vehemently opposed to backing up onto floppies; see "Floppy Mania" in "Backing Up," later in this book.

I didn't say I don't want a floppy disk drive for my notebook, mind you; I just said I don't want it *built in*. Increasingly, savvy PC manufacturers are throwing a separate, external floppy drive into the box with every notebook they produce, instead of making it a separate, expensive, after-sale add-on. That cuts the effective cost of an external floppy dramatically—because the company makes so many more—and it makes good sense. NEC pioneered this good business practice with its Ultralite III; other vendors are picking up on the idea.

In truth, you really don't need a floppy disk drive at all for a notebook. Many notebooks now come with a file-transfer program, such as Travelling Software's excellent LapLink, built into the machine's ROM memory, or at least as a free software package included in the box with the machine.

LapLink, HotWire, FastLynx and a number of other, similar file-transfer programs can free you entirely from the tyranny of floppy disk drives on portable computers by letting you connect the portable to a desktop machine via the package's cable, then run the program on both machines, moving files back and forth with ease. LapLink, in fact, even checks first to see if a copy of the program is installed on the other computer when you first make the connection; if not, it automatically installs itself on that machine, then goes to work.

I use and like LapLink; friends use and prefer other transfer programs. All work well.

But as easy as they are to use, they still aren't as easy as simply moving files between two machines via a floppy disk. So I fall back on the external floppy drive for my notebook PC as the *really* quick and easy way to move a file or two.

When I have lots of files to transfer—maybe a whole subdirectory's worth—I always use LapLink. It's crazy to keep shuffling a floppy back and forth, back and forth. If the data I need to move won't fit on a single 1.44 MB floppy, then by definition I think it's too much data to move via floppies. Back to LapLink.

So—there are my arguments against buying a notebook PC with a built-in floppy-disk drive.

My friends who do like floppy drives in notebooks offer the following arguments:

- **They feel more secure when they have a floppy drive available.** (Is this a '90s update of Linus's security blanket?)
- **They often swap files with people they meet on the street when they're travelling.** (Weird . . . but OK, I'll take their word for it.)
- **They like to do backups at night when they travel.** (Confirms your worst fears, doesn't it, about the kinds of people who write for and edit computer magazines? Boy, we're a lot of fun on the road.)
- **They know they'd just lose an external floppy-disk drive.** (They said it, I didn't. But I think they're probably right on this one; self-knowledge can be a wonderful yet terrible thing.)

I rest my case. You don't want an internal floppy-disk drive in your notebook PC. But you do want an external drive, which should live in your desk drawer, not in your travelling bag.

Pointing Devices

Here's another choice that really comes down to personal preference—though from the way some people argue about it, you'd think it was a matter of life and death.

If you use Windows, you have to have some kind of pointing device for positioning the cursor. If you use a relatively few other, non-Windows programs that make good use of a pointing device—Microsoft Word 5.0 and Quattro Pro 4.0 come immediately to mind—you'll probably also want a pointing gizmo, though it isn't quite so important. (And if you neither use Windows nor run any DOS programs that support pointing devices, you can safely skip ahead to the next chapter.)

The usual pointing device for a computer is a mouse. And for years, I carried a conventional Logitech mouse with me when I travelled; plugged into the serial port on my laptop PC of the moment, it was an invaluable help when I was running a program such as Word. On airplanes, I'd simply roll the mouse around atop my right thigh—there's rarely enough room for both PC and mouse on those dinky little fold-down or pull-up trays the airlines provide—and that, you may be sure, drew some *verrrry* strange glances from seatmates and small children sitting across the aisle.

In those days, laptop PCs were novelty enough; computer mice weren't much seen outside places like Microsoft.

Today, I use a Microsoft BallPoint or a Logitech TrackMan Portable instead. These are two remarkably similar devices, both developed at the same time, in great secrecy, and first announced and shown on almost the same day—to the horror of the two design teams, who wondered aloud how the competition could possibly have come up with something so similar. Both clip onto the right-hand side of the computer, and offer a small trackball.

I find trackballs more useful and appealing, generally, than standard mice, because of their superior ergonomics and better accuracy. Never used a trackball? Think of it as an upside-down mouse, with the ball on the top, where you roll it around with the palm of your hand or your fingertips, rather than on the bottom, where it rolls on the desktop while you move the much greater mass of the mouse with your hand.

Portable trackballs, such as the Microsoft and Logitech entries, bring the base of the unit up off the table, and allow you to position the ball at an angle, rather than rolling it horizontally.

The most comfortable way to use either of these "road mice" is to cup them in your right hand, then use the side of your thumb to roll the trackball back and forth. Both offer angle adjustments; I leave mine at about 45 degrees. The equivalent of a mouse's left and right click-buttons lie on the edge of the units, where it's easy to press them with your right index finger and thumb.

Both take a little getting used to. I was at first put off by them, and for a time after they were introduced, I went back and forth between them and a conventional mouse. That experience taught me their merits; now I always use one of these tiny trackballs when I travel.

You'll have to experiment to find the right attachment point and angle. If your notebook PC has a floppy disk drive mounted on its right side, near the front—a common location—then you'll have to either slide the mouse further back towards the back of the PC, or forsake use of the floppy drive while the mouse is attached. I choose the latter.

There's a good alternative to the Logitech and Microsoft travelling mice, but it's not something you can buy and add on. The Isopoint is a remarkable rolling cylinder, mounted by a few notebook PC manufacturers in the front edge of their notebooks' housing, just in front of the spacebar. A small tab on the cylinder slides back and forth, so you have both lateral motion and rolling motion, which lets you position the cursor anywhere on screen with a simple movement of either thumb.

I really love Isopoints, and it's a shame the idea has not caught on more widely.

An Isopoint-equipped PC has to be a little deeper from front to back to accommodate the mechanism, and of course the idea of a rolling-bar "mouse" at first seems odd. Vendors don't like to do missionary work, so the Isopoint has not been widely adopted. The best implementation of it that I've seen is on an otherwise-undistinguished GRiD Systems notebook.

The Isopoint isn't so good that it's worth basing your whole buying decision on whether a machine has one—you'd have to forsake too many other important features, especially since it has been used in so few machines—but if you notice a machine with an Isopoint in a computer store someday, stop and play with it. You'll wish *your* notebook had one.

Two other interesting alternatives to the Logitech and Microsoft mice—and, of course, to traditional computer mice and trackballs, as well—come from Appoint. One, the PenMouse, is a clumsy, stick-like device you hold upright, just as you would a pen. You manipulate the cursor position onscreen by, in effect, "drawing" with the unit, rolling its tip round on a horizontal surface.

I don't think much of the PenMouse. It's like holding a fat MagicMarker in your hand, and I dislike constantly picking it up and putting it down. It's an ungainly solution, and a slow way to work.

Appoint makes yet another oddball pointing device for portable PCs which I do like very much, however. Their Thumbelina is a flat pad about an inch-and-a-half square, which can be mounted anywhere you wish—though most Thumbelina users hang it on the right side of their notebook PCs, much like the Logitech and Microsoft units.

It has a truly tiny trackball-like roller-ball emerging from its surface—the ball is about the size of a pea—plus the usual buttons.

I find the Thumbelina irksome when I try to use it as a standard mouse, but it's invaluable as a "remote-control" mouse for presenters. When you're running a PC slide show, whether showing the material to an audience of one or two on the built-in screen of your portable, or feeding the image out through the machine's external video jack to a projector of one sort or another, using any sort of conventional mouse is nearly hopeless.

But the Thumbelina is absolutely perfect for presentations. You can hide it in your hand, much like a 35mm Carousel projector's remote control, and use it to advance your "slides," move a cursor onscreen like a laser-pointer, and control the show almost as if by magic.

The Thumbelina's cord, which is too long for ordinary use, is perfect, too, for these situations: you don't need to keep your "mouse hand" right next to the keyboard.

Finally, a few notebook PCs are beginning to appear with conventional trackballs submerged in their keyboards, to the right of the alphanumeric keys. Trackballs built into keyboards have never enjoyed much success on standard PCs, and I'm skeptical that these built-in pointing devices will survive very long in portables, either.

But anyone who's used one of Apple's PowerBook Macintosh portables immediately understands the usefulness and comfort of a built-in trackball. The Mac's absolute reliance on a pointing device as a primary input system forced Apple's designers to experiment with the idea, and they came up with a winner.

Perhaps the Apple ergonomic research, which produced a relatively large, centrally mounted trackball that lies between the front of the computer and the keyboard, will prove useful to a PC vendor, who'll risk a similarly bold and innovative solution in a DOS/Windows notebook PC.

Carrying Cases

It strikes me as odd that so few makers of laptop and notebook PCs offer decent cases for their machines. Laptop PCs tend to be relatively bulky and fragile—a perfect description of something that needs a case for safe transport. Notebook PCs almost always come without handles, have flat, slippery sides, and are relatively fragile—another good description of something that cries out for a carrying case.

So why are computer makers' cases so poor?

Few computer cases have room for anything but the computer, for example. Some have recesses or pockets for such accessories as AC power supplies and power cords, but especially with a small, lightweight notebook PC, those are better carried in a suitcase, or simply left at your desk if you're just carrying the computer down the hall to a meeting.

And what about the *non*-computer stuff we carry along? Newspapers? Magazines? Paperwork? File folders? Passports? Airline tickets and itineraries? Address books? Filofaxes and DayRunners? A Walkman or Discman, maybe, with a tiny headset?

I think there are two viable models for computer cases. There's the minimalist approach—a slim, lightweight nylon carrying case just about the size of the computer itself. You can slip the PC into it along, perhaps, with a couple of floppies and maybe a half-dozen sheets of letter-sized paper. This version's ideal for the quick trip to a meeting down the hall or across town.

Then there's the true Road Warrior case, the one that holds not only the computer itself, but all that paraphernalia I mentioned a minute ago.

This is the one for out-of-town trips, for slogging along with all that paperwork you'll need to use when you work with the computer and everything else you'll need to take your desk on the road.

It's not quite fair to say no computer maker offers good cases. Dell, for example, offers two computer cases of exactly the kinds I've described for most of their machines. There's a lightweight, flimsy nylon stuff-case that's just right for the computer itself, and a fatter, small-gym-bag alternative with room for the kitchen sink. Dell's larger cases are usually made from very good soft vinyl or leather; you wouldn't be embarrassed carrying one into Buckingham Palace.

But that's the end of the list. Toshiba has in the past offered good laptop and notebook PC cases, but their present offerings are pretty thin. Compaq, IBM, and Zenith have all produced the occasional well-designed case, but the good ones disappear from the product line quickly, it seems, to be replaced by newer models which make me wonder if their designers have ever *seen* a portable PC, let alone carried one on the road for a few days.

Happily, there is a booming third-party aftermarket in portable computer cases. Much of this is shlock, goods you wouldn't take for free. But some independent makers' products are very, very good, better than anything I've seen from a computer maker.

The very best portable PC cases I've found come from Targus. Their Premier model is my current favorite. A classy leather case in the form of a traditional lawyer's briefcase, it accommodates even the largest laptop PC, plus pencils, pens, calculator, business cards, floppy disks, newspapers, magazines, reports, and other paperwork. I carry a relatively small notebook PC in mine; the extra space left over after I've put the notebook in accommodates a thin Toshiba CD player, a few CDs and a set of headphones, and an NEC cellular phone.

Best of all, perhaps, is that unlike most computer cases, which scream *Computer Geek! Computer Geek!* when you walk through an airport or into someone's office, the Targus Premier is a classy-looking *business* case, in black leather, without a hint of its computer-case role.

Targus has other interesting cases, as well, some of which are also available from computer makers, on an OEM basis. Their Universal notebook case is ideal for the notebook user who also wants to carry along a small, flat printer, such as the Canon BubbleJet. Its two-tier design accommodates the notebook PC on one side, and the printer on the other, in an identical, 11 × 13 × 2 1/2-inch compartment. This is also a good case for the PC-plus-fax-machine traveller. There isn't much room left for paperwork, magazines, and other miscellany, but the Universal does a good job of transporting and protecting the computer and printer.

These are all soft-side cases, in the current fashion. Another approach comes from Samsonite, Solidex, and others, who sell semi-rigid shell-type cases. The idea here is that you get greater shock-resistance in a hard-shell case, which is true enough. But I find these cases, as a class, less convenient, less attractive, and generally pretty clumsy.

That said, Solidex's K325 and K315X, two of their smaller models, are nicely made and functional. If you worry about dropping your computer case—or about someone stacking a 40-pound box atop it after you've put it in an overhead bin on an airliner—take a look at these designs.

You don't *need* an "official computer carrying case" for your PC, of course. My machines often travel in one of three wonderful older business cases of mine: an ancient Hartmann belting-leather case that looks like it's been through a war (and is the handsomer for it); a gorgeous brown-leather Scully bag from Italy; and an engagingly beat-up Orvis fishing bag.

It wasn't possible to stick your portable PC into a conventional business case back in the early days of the Compaq luggables, of course, nor was it very practical to stick many of the early laptops in one: it would have filled the case, leaving room for nothing else. And maybe have ripped the bottom out of the case when you lifted it. But today's small notebook PCs can be tucked into almost any conventional case, with room left over for the other business tools you carry.

And Some Esoterica . . .

There's a world of add-on doodads and accessories for portable PCs. Just as with desktop computers, the shlock factor is pretty high: a lot of this stuff has little use for *anyone*. But there's wheat among this chaff, and if you have special needs, some of these add-ons may prove genuinely useful.

Herewith some notes on some of the more worthwhile system extensions I've found for notebook and laptop PCs.

Portable Hard Disks

Sometimes you need more disk space because you've simply filled up the built-in hard disk on your PC. That happens often to Windows users, for example: 20 MB and 40 MB hard disks were never meant for Windows' 5 MB and 6 MB applications, nor for Windows' own space-gobbling storage needs.

But there are other reasons you might want to add more hard-disk capacity to your portable PC. I know a number of PC users, for example, who carry large and frequently updated databases with them when they travel. In a few cases, the data is stored on company-produced CD-ROM disks, which are updated every few weeks or months. These people carry portable CD-ROM players with them, along with their notebook PCs (keep reading for more on CD-ROMs on the road).

Others, however, use databases that are updated too frequently for CD-ROM pressings, and so use the data in magnetic form, on external hard disks. Some could easily fit the information onto the disks in their portable PCs, but prefer the convenience of segregating that data onto an external disk. That way they can simply leave the external disk in the office for the day when it's being updated, without having to leave their PCs behind, too.

Finally, compact external hard disks make excellent transfer media for very large quantities of data. A company I work with uses a fleet of portable hard disks to carry highly confidential design and contract information around the country. Their "Johnny Appleseed" users then can download all or part of the data to the PCs of colleagues with whom they're working, wherever they are—or *not* download it, but simply attach the external disk to those PCs for the period they need access to the information—thus helping defeat unwanted copying and dissemination of the data.

Once, portable external hard disks were rare birds, indeed. Today, though, as we've learned to use two-way parallel printer ports more wisely, tiny portable hard disks, some of which have their own battery supplies for use away from power lines, are becoming widely available.

Parallel-port connections are critical here: how else would we quickly and easily establish a high-speed link between the disk and our expansion-slotless PC? (A SCSI adapter, such as Trantor's MiniSCSI, would also work, but adds unnecessary cost to the system, if all you want to do is pipeline hard-disk data back and forth.)

I've tried several tiny portable hard disks; the best I've seen are the Flashdrive 25 units from BSE. These are state-of-the-art $2^{1}/_{2}$-inch IDE (integrated drive electronics) hard drives, cleverly repackaged to make them into portable, battery-powered, self-contained travelling units. I always warn PC users that *all* hard disks, whether "packed to go" or not, are relatively fragile, and thus could lose critical data—but I've bounced my Flashdrive around a lot, and never lost a byte. BSE pays special attention to drive design and drive ruggedness when choosing components, with the result that the finished units are remarkably tough.

Flashdrives are available in capacities ranging from 20 to 130 MB. My current favorite uses a new, US-made Toshiba 85 MB $2^{1}/_{2}$-inch drive. This Toshiba drive has extremely low power requirements, very high shock resistance, and extremely rugged glass platters. All in all, it's a superb choice for a portable unit. BSE packs that drive, plus the interface electronics and power supply, into a small black-plastic cabinet 5 × 5 × $1^1/2$ inches that weighs just a shade over a pound.

Using Flashdrives is simplicity itself. Just plug one end of the cable (provided with the drive) into the drive's COMPUTER connector, and the other end of that cable into your PC's printer port. If you want to have your printer available, plug the printer cable you removed from your PC into the Flashdrive's PRINTER connector. That's it. The first time you use the system you need to run an install program, which simply sets the default time-out on the hard drive's batteries—the period after which it will shut down, to avoid running down the batteries—and also copies a tiny 1,500-byte driver file to your PC's disk.

Flashdrives are not particularly cheap—this is not an easy trick to pull off, and the high-quality drive components are costly—but neither are they exorbitantly expensive. BSE's 20 MB drive lists for $299, my 85 MB runs $799, and a 130 MB unit costs $899. Those are list prices; BSE's relatively few dealers typically discount them by about 20 percent. Note that only about 20 percent of BSE's drives go out under their own name; they OEM portable, battery-powered drives to a number of other vendors, under whose label you may be able to find better prices.

Like almost everything else in this list, these aren't for everyone. But if you've outgrown your portable PC's internal hard disk and don't want to (or can't) replace it, or if you occasionally need to carry around large quantities of data you don't want to (or can't) copy onto your machine's internal disk, these are tools worth considering.

CD-ROM Drives

Portable CD-ROM players are still uncommon, but you'll see more and more of them on the market over the next year or so. One force driving their emergence has been the explosion in proprietary, privately produced CD-ROM disks, published by corporations for internal use. Some of these disks are little more than glorified parts lists (still, a valid and cost-effective use of the technology); others function as up-to-the-minute catalogs, with easily updated pricing. Some are compendia of proprietary technical data, such as the drilling and site-data disks published by an oil company I've worked with.

All of these disks—and of course the growing number of commercially published reference disks as well, such as Lotus's extensive financial-data disk series, and the Sheshunoff banking-industry information—are now accessible to you on the road with a portable CD player.

The first portable CD-ROM drive, NEC's CDR-35, was something of a dog—slow and clumsy. NEC made great strides with its successor, the Intersect CDR-36, which is a very useful tool. Access times still don't match the fastest desktop units—on average, the CDR-36 takes twice as long to find a piece of information as do the better desktop units—so you probably don't want one of these portables on your desk as your only CD-ROM machine.

But for travel, the CDR-36 is a joy. And at about $450 at typical street prices, it's a bargain. If you need access to CD-ROM data when you're travelling, this is the drive to buy.

Keyboard Extensions

Accountants, it is said, love separate, external numeric keypads for their portable PCs. These cigarette-pack-sized extensions plug into your machine, then sit to the right of your keyboard, where they function just like the numeric keypad of a desktop PC, when the NumLock key is turned on.

I work closely with a number of large accounting firms on their computer problems, and for years I've been looking for accountants who really do use these things. So far, I've found maybe a dozen. Most, it seems, are content to live with the "embedded" keypads built into portables' keyboards.

Actually, "content" is the wrong word. When I ask about this, accountants (and others who do a lot of numeric entry) scream and yell about the inconvenience of using embedded keypads, which require holding down a "Fn," or function key, to activate them. But when I ask if they've tried an external keypad—and sometimes, when I have one with me and pull it out for them to see and try—they quickly decide they'd rather live with the inconveniences of an embedded keypad, rather than haul one more thing around with them.

So this may be a question of temperament as much as it is of real need. If you enter a lot of numbers, and hate to have to remember to hold down the other key that activates the embedded keys, then take a look at external numeric keypads. They're available for almost all of the major brands of notebook and laptop PCs, from the makers of those machines.

For the few machines whose vendors don't offer external keypads, third-party firms make generic add-on keypads which serve the same purpose. I recommend the units sold by Genovation, which avoid compatibility problems by attaching to the PC's parallel printer port (and pass the printer connector through, so you can have both the keypad and printer attached and active at the same time).

Megabatteries

I used to find battery-replacement cords and packs, which let you power your computer from, say, a car's cigarette lighter socket, or away from all power sources, when you're deep in the jungle, ludicrous. And the accessory, clip-on battery packs that let you keep computing after your machine's internal batteries have pooped out were almost as funny.

Then I spoke with officers on a large state patrol force, who use notebook PCs constantly in their police cruisers, and who run the units all the time from the cars' cigarette-lighter jacks. And then I spoke with anthropologists, who do work in the jungle, where they use a solar system to charge external batteries, from which they then run their portable PCs.

And then I started using a clip-on battery unit for my own PC, for long flights.

I may not always get things right the first time, but at least I'm trainable: I was wrong. Not everyone needs these external-power systems—but if you do, you need 'em bad.

I'm now really taken by add-on battery packs. I have and use two different kinds. One, designed by Sharp and Texas Instruments, is a clip-on "slice" which mounts very elegantly across the back of a laptop PC I own. It supplements the internal batteries in that computer, upping their working life from two hours to five. That's long enough for cross-country flights, and with an extra one of these "slices," I can get across the Atlantic or Pacific on batteries. (No, I don't usually work 10 hours straight on airplanes; but I do often work a great deal of the time on these long, boring flights. At least I do *now,* since I have enough battery power to keep the computer running as long as *I'm* running.)

A second, more powerful battery pack from Cuesta Systems powers another portable computer I own. It's a beast—5 × 8 × 2 inches thick, and about eight pounds—so I don't carry it everywhere. But I do use it when I'm going to be at a fixed but powerless location for a day and hope to get some work done while I'm there. I've used it in mountain cabins, at the beach, and on construction sites where power lines hadn't yet been set up.

There's always a trade-off here, between going to one of these oddball external power supplies and simply buying an extra battery or two for your machine. As batteries get smaller, lighter, and more powerful—the new generation of nickel-hydride PC batteries, for example—that becomes a better solution. But if you have an older machine, for which extra batteries are large and clumsy—or are simply unavailable—or if you use a PC in a car or boat for long hours, consider external battery power supplies and "card cords."

They're useful, if highly specialized, tools.

Cellular Phone Connections

It seems so logical to use a cellular phone link for PC communications. That would avoid the problems of hooking into someone else's telephone system; it would make PC communications completely independent of fixed locations and AC power supplies.

In real life, hooking up your PC to a cellular connection isn't as easy as it should be, but it may still be worth the trouble.

The basic problem is the cellular system's architecture. As you may know, cellular systems work with our very low-powered cellular phones by dotting an area with many low-power radio repeating stations. As you drive across town talking on your car phone, your call is more-or-less invisibly switched from one of these stations, or cells, to the next, and then to the next, and then to the next.

With each switch there is a brief break in the connection, as one repeating station hands off your call to the next. You usually don't notice, and your phone conversation almost always continues uninterrupted.

Now try that while driving across town, using your portable PC and modem, connected through that same car phone to the cellular system.

Those occasional breaks in the connection are a disaster for the PC: the modem thinks the line has been dropped, and shuts down, assuming you're through with the call.

But what, you may say, about the convenience of using a PC and modem with a cellular connection when you're sitting still—at a remote site, for example, without land-line phone service?

Here you're still at risk, because of the automatic load-balancing switching performed by the cellular system. Smart software watches the traffic passing through each cell. When the load from callers' cellular telephones on that cell's receiver/transmitter becomes high—which could freeze-out other users trying to place calls—the system automatically looks for an adjacent cell that is being underused. If it finds one, it flips your call over to that other cell. This is possible because, at any given moment, cellular phone users are typically within reach of three or four cells' repeating stations: the nearest one, plus others which, though slightly more distant, are still workable.

As valuable as this kind of load-balancing is to keeping the cellular system up and running, it's murder on PC communications: even when you're sitting still, you may still get knocked off the air.

New cellular modems are available that can tolerate these interruptions in carrier signals. They perform the usual error-checking and required retransmissions when working normally; then when the data stream is interrupted because of a cell change, they simply check to see what was lost during the lapsed connection and retransmit the missing data. And they do *not* hang up on you during hand-offs. The key here has been Microcom's new MNP-10 communications protocol, which manages the hand-off and data-retransmission.

How valuable cellular modems may be to you depends on just how much you need to stay in touch via your PC. Tooling around town in the back seat of a limo, checking your e-mail as you go, may be a nice Hollywood screenwriter's trick, but has little applicability for most of us. Yet if you do need to transmit data from a remote location with no land-line service—or if you need to send and receive information from sites where connecting to the existing telephone system presents problems—cellular modems can make a great deal of sense.

Just as cellular service itself is not especially cheap, cellular modems also are not inexpensive; you'll spend $1,200–$1,500 or so for a good one.

My favorite so far is Mitsubishi's M1500, which combines a standard cellular telephone with an MNP-10-capable data modem. Models are available which mount permanently in an automobile, or which can be carried anywhere, with your laptop or notebook PC. The transportable version's ni-cad batteries allow about 15 hours of standby time, and up to an hour-and-a-half of talking or data-transmission time.

They're expensive by usual modem-pricing standards, but cellular modems can solve devilishly difficult PC communications problems. And using them is fun: you'll find it hard to suppress a giggle the first time you make a data call from your PC to your office—while you're sitting in a folding chair at the edge of a lake.

A Notebook Software Kit

One easy answer to the question "What software should I put on my portable PC?" is . . . EVERYthing. Everything, that is, that you have installed on the hard disk in your desktop PC. But unless you've found a way to stuff a desktop-PC-sized hard disk into that notebook, that's impossible: it won't all fit.

That's not really a problem, since a lot of the programs on your desktop PC's hard disk have probably been there for years without being run. The key to portable computing is to pick the just-right software kit: what you need to get the job done, no more, and certainly not that illegal copy of a French database manager your brother-in-law gave you in 1987, or the copy you made of your kid's copy of Wheel of Fortune, Vanna's Silver Anniversary Edition.

DOS or Windows?

Are you going to run strictly DOS, and DOS applications, on your notebook or laptop, or are you going to run Windows as well? That's a critical decision, because it shapes the kind of portable PC you should buy and its hardware configuration (see "The Windows Question," in "Sorting Out Portable PCs"), the kind of remote-control software you should choose, if you want to run a desktop PC in your office from your portable when you're away from your desk (see "The Windows Issue" in "Remote Computing"), and the kinds of applications software you should put on the portable, which we'll talk about here.

There is a half-simple rule of thumb at work here: If you're running Windows and Windows applications on your desktop PC, then you should also run Windows and those same Windows applications on your notebook or laptop, whether you see the portable machine as an extension of your desktop computer or as a replacement for it. With the possible exceptions of a simple, on-the-go word-processor such as Eye Relief (keep reading), and a simple communications program for e-mail, once you've learned and become accustomed to Windows-style computing on your main PC, you'll go nuts trying to move back and forth between a set of DOS applications on the travelling machine and a set of Windows programs on your desktop.

The most obvious problems—the need to remember different commands, a different directory and subdirectory structure, and other operational issues—aren't the half of it. The real problem is that you won't be able to move files back and forth between the DOS and Windows universes without some hassle.

No matter how loudly Windows applications vendors claim that their products can transparently convert DOS applications' files to the Windows program's format—and then reconvert them after you've worked on those files in the other environment—the conversion process just doesn't work that well. I can promise you THERE WILL BE GLITCHES.

But even if those round trips did work as reliably and invisibly as advertised, you'd be crazy to put up with that constant shuttling of files back and forth. Why wait for, say, Word for Windows to read in a DOS Word 5.0 file, or a WordPerfect 5.1 file, before you can go to work? And why bother saving a second, alien-format version of each file you may want to move to the other environment?

Make life simple: If you run Windows on one of your PCs, run it on both (or all) of your PCs.

Until recently, that wasn't realistic, of course. When 80286-based portables were the state of the art, 20 MB hard disks ruled the portable world, and 1 MB of RAM expandable (at substantial expense) to 2 MB was the norm for portables, using Windows on them made no sense. Now, happily, with 386SX and better machines dominating the portable-PC landscape, Windows-to-go makes a lot of sense—*if* you're a Windows fan.

But I said that rule of thumb was only half-simple. It prescribes what you should do if you use Windows already on a primary machine but what do you do if you *don't* use Windows? The obverse—if you don't use Windows at your desk, DON'T use it on the road—isn't necessarily right.

Many PC users these days find themselves on the cusp between the DOS world and the Windows world. They've seen and played with Windows; they think Windows 3.1 and its higher-powered successor, Windows *NT,* look pretty good, and they're seriously considering a changeover.

If that describes you, then maybe the time to change to Windows is as you move to a new notebook or laptop PC. If it's to be your only PC, the decision is easier; if you're still going to split your computing time between a desktop machine and a portable, you want to avoid getting caught up in the different-systems trap I described a minute ago.

An interim step many users find worthwhile is to put Windows on their portable PC, but to duplicate only their standard DOS applications on the machine. Then, for the first few months, they use Windows simply as a context-switching utility. That is, they run their standard DOS application programs for a while under Windows, then gradually begin adding true Windows applications to replace those DOS apps.

In the past I've argued against this kind of two-step conversion to Windows, so I owe you an explanation of my change of heart. It seemed to me—and on one level, seems to me still—that if you're going to put your toe in the water with Windows, you may as well go all the way, with Windows applications as well. Otherwise you're only getting a small fraction of the benefits of Windows and a graphical interface in general—but still paying the whole, steep price of using Windows, in terms of its learning curve and robust hardware requirements.

But Windows 3.1 changed my mind. I still think that for those who are persuaded to jump into Windows, going whole-hog with Windows applications too makes a lot of sense. But Windows 3.1 is such a good memory-manager and applications-switcher that it has real benefits even for those who plan to rely, if only on an interim basis, on standard DOS applications. And since learning Windows' own way of working—using ALT + TAB to switch among several programs running at the same time, for example, or getting used to mice and pull-down menus—takes a while, making the move in two steps lets the new Windows user become comfortable with the conventions of the environment before plunging into the additional vagaries of Windows applications.

For many PC users, moving to a notebook PC—or moving up to an up-to-date, fully powered notebook after years of working with earlier, clunky, severely compromised laptops—opens a new door to a wider use of the computer in their business days and possibly in their personal lives, too. Opening that door even wider by moving to Windows at the same time makes the journey even more rewarding.

System Level: DOS and Memory Managers

Most new notebook and laptop users set up their systems very much like they've set up their desktop PCs. If the two hardware configurations are very similar, and if the desktop machine has been highly optimized for the most efficient use of memory, processor cycles, hard disk space and so on, then that's a good idea. But even in these days of mega-portables, portable versus desktop configurations are rarely that close—and in practice, desktop PCs are rarely truly optimized for their installed resources.

Dealing with issues such as efficient allocation of memory, saving battery power, and making the most of an LCD screen are so important in setting up a portable PC that mimicking the setup of a desktop machine almost always produces less than the best results on the portable.

We'll look at several areas in which your choice of system-level options can make, collectively, a big difference in the performance of your portable, and the pleasure of using it, beginning with your choice of an operating system and a memory manager.

The brand and version of DOS installed on your portable PC can make a substantial difference in the memory available for running application programs and in overall system performance. I use Microsoft MS-DOS

5.0 on the portables I use regularly, and haven't had cause to regret that decision.

Actually, of course, it was an easy decision, almost a non-decision, because MS-DOS itself, and now especially version 5.0, is the overwhelming standard. So I was hardly going out on a limb. But my reservations about earlier releases of Microsoft's flagship product—especially the notorious DOS 4.0 and 4.01—made it a less-than-automatic choice. Like a lot of savvy PC users, I stayed with the rock-solid MS-DOS releases 3.1 and 3.3 long after they'd been superseded by later versions. But DOS 5.0 offers significant advantages, and has proved even more reliable than earlier versions.

The principal reason to install DOS 5.0 is that in almost any configuration it takes up less RAM than earlier versions and for users of 386SX and 386DX machines and higher, spending a little time tweaking DOS 5.0's settings can reward you with a system that takes up even less of that precious 640 KB of RAM available to applications. This involves judicious use of DOS 5.0's HIMEM memory manager, which ships selected chunks of program code off to so-called "high memory"—that block of RAM between 640 KB and 1 MB normally reserved for such system-level functions as video memory.

Using high memory is hardly a new idea, and DOS 5.0 is neither the best nor the most flexible tool for addressing unused and fragmented high memory. Qualitas' 386/MAX and Quarterdeck's QEMM-386 are both superior tools, and with some effort on the user's part they can wring out even more free memory in that critical first 640 KB of RAM. But many portable PC users tell me they're perfectly happy with the amount of memory recovered through the use of DOS 5.0's DOS=HIGH commands under HIMEM, and it's true that HIMEM can often do almost as good a job of reclaiming memory as the Qualitas or Quarterdeck products. If the extra 15–50 KB you can usually recover through using one of these add-on utilities rather than HIMEM isn't worth the trouble of installing them and going through their set-up and optimization routines—not to mention paying their typical $60 – $70 price tags—then why bother?

The memory-saving advantages of MS-DOS 5.0 come only with that version (and presumably, with later releases), and reach their fullest expression only with PCs using 386SX and higher microprocessors. While you can use utilities to gain some of the memory-saving benefits of MS-DOS 5.0 with earlier versions of Microsoft's DOS and on 286-based PCs, it makes more sense to upgrade to MS-DOS 5.0 first, then add those utilities only if you feel you still need them.

An interesting alternative to Microsoft's MS-DOS 5.0 is DR DOS 6.0 from Digital Research, now a division of Novell, the LAN software company. Digital Research tweaked the Redmond giant's nose hard when it rolled out DR DOS 5.0 while Microsoft was still selling MS-DOS 4.0 with all its warts. DR DOS anticipated many of the features in MS-DOS 5.0; indeed, many observers believe its features were adopted overnight by Microsoft as a kind of panicked "DOS fixes" list for the development of MS-DOS 5.0.

When Digital Research then rolled out DR DOS 6.0 not long after Microsoft shipped MS-DOS 5.0, the contest was on again. Digital Research's acquisition shortly thereafter by Novell was a delicious turn for PC-industry watchers, for it suggested an inevitable, full-scale confrontation between Novell, which had already whipped Microsoft in the network-software business, and Microsoft. Novell seems certain to confront Redmond head-to-head in the DOS arena as well.

But while DR DOS 5.0 and 6.0 are interesting products and work well, I find no compelling reason to change to them. I've worked with both extensively and have found no serious compatibility problems or other glitches; they're good products. But absent a compelling reason to change—as opposed to minor, tweaky advantages I may never use—staying with MS-DOS fits my oft-repeated prescription for keeping life simple.

Having mentioned 386/MAX and QEMM-386, and having said they're both better and more sophisticated memory managers than DOS's own tools, I can't end this chapter with that little tease unresolved. I greatly admire both products, and if you're interested in twiddling and tweaking a little, both can be rewarding additions to your computer toolkit.

Both programs exploit the memory-management tricks built-into Intel's 386SX and higher microprocessors (and into the 386 and higher clone chips from AMD, Cyrix, and other vendors). Both can sniff around in that messy block of RAM between 640 KB and 1 MB, find discontiguous fragments of memory left unused by your system, and knit that memory together in a way that makes those blocks large enough to be usable. Like DOS's HIMEM, they can then fit small programs—utilities, DOS's COMMAND.COM interpreter, network software, little "loader" code modules which call larger terminate-and-stay-resident programs into action—into that recovered memory. By relocating these chunks of code out of the base 640 KB and up into this formerly wasted high memory, they can make a remarkable difference in the amount of memory left in that 640 KB block to run your application programs.

Rules of thumb are tricky here, but if the average PC user might wind up with, say 550 KB of RAM left from that 640 KB after using DOS 5.0's HIMEM and DOS=HIGH tricks, a savvy user of 386/MAX or QEMM-386 might wind up with 575 KB to perhaps as much as 610 KB left for applications.

Both 386/MAX and QEMM-386 were reasonably cranky in their earlier versions, requiring a lot of twiddling and experimenting to get something like the optimum combination of slices of code swapped up to high memory. Current versions of both programs are much easier to use, and in some cases, their installation routines make nearly optimal relocation of code almost automatic. But the very nature of twiddly high-memory managers encourages users to do their own fine-tuning, and it's easy to find you've spent an afternoon trying to wring an extra 3 KB of base memory out of your setup.

Thus as much as I like these programs—of the two, I prefer 386/MAX, and have it installed on some of the computers I use—I urge you to see what you can do with DOS 5.0's HIMEM utility first. If it doesn't recover enough memory for you, or you find it difficult to use, or you simply realize how much you like playing around with system settings on your PC—by all means take a look at 386/MAX or QEMM-386.

For the portable PC user who demands the last ounce of optimization and performance, they're splendid tools. For the rest of us, HIMEM will probably do just fine, thanks.

Disk Caching

Few gains in performance in the computer world come so easily and so cheaply as setting aside a large block of RAM to serve as a disk cache. Performance is much snappier, and notebook and laptop owners get an additional bonus in the form of longer battery life.

To understand why disk caches are so important for portable-PC users, and to make the most of the one you install, it helps to know a little about how disk caches work.

When an application program running on your PC needs a new chunk of information—a piece of program code not normally resident in memory, but swapped in and out of memory only as needed (such as a dictionary or thesaurus), or a piece of data for one of your documents (such as the contents of page 62 of your proposal for a new operating division)—the program tells the PC to look up that data on the hard disk, read it, and transfer it to RAM, where the program can use it.

Because that involves an electro-mechanical *seek-find-read* process, it's much slower than if the retrieval of data were, like most of the computational processes in your PC, entirely electronic. Using a disk-caching program goes a long way towards achieving that goal of making the data-retrieval process entirely electronic.

When you install a disk caching program (by simply copying it to your PC's hard disk, then adding a line to your CONFIG.SYS file), you set aside a specified block of the memory installed in your PC exclusively for disk caching. Thereafter, when a program asks for the next piece of data from the hard disk, the computer looks first in this cache-memory RAM, which serves as a kind of temporary holding pen for data. Only if it cannot be found there does the PC have to make the much slower trip to the hard disk to find the information and read it into RAM.

The first time the PC looks into the cache after you've loaded an application program, it doesn't find anything, because the caching program doesn't yet know what to put there. But after that first data request is serviced by a trip to the disk, the caching program takes over and begins working invisibly, behind the scenes, filling the cache with the data it thinks you're probably going to ask for next. It bases those guesses on how the data is stored on the hard disk, and what you've just asked for. For example, it might read in the next few clusters of data from the file, following the one in which the data from your first request was found.

Thus every time thereafter your application asks for more data, the PC looks first in this holding pond set up by the caching program. If the data is found there, it's instantly transferred to working RAM, where the program can begin using it. Only when the data is not in the cache must the PC begin the usual hunt for it on the hard disk.

As the cache "overflows," it is flushed according to one of several algorithms that attempt to increase cache effectiveness. Under LRU flushing, for example, the least-recently-used data is flushed to make room for new data the caching program thinks you may want next.

Cache efficiency can be astonishingly high; good cache programs are very accurate at guessing what you'll need next. The effectiveness of a cache is also determined by the size of the block of RAM you set aside for it: obviously, the application program is much more likely to be able to find what it needs if you've set up a 2 MB cache than if you've set up a 16 KB cache. But with a well-designed program and a reasonable cache size, you can expect to avoid 90 percent or more of the trips you'd otherwise make to the disk.

The best disk-caching program available is Super PC-Kwik, from Multisoft. At less than $100 at typical street prices, Super PC-Kwik provides an amazing kick in the pants for your computer at relatively low cost. Current versions work equally well with both DOS and DOS with Windows.

Of course, you may need to add more RAM to use a caching program effectively, so that may add to the cost of setting up a cache. In the past, most users used very small caches, on the order of 32 KB to 64 KB. In part that was because RAM was a precious thing, and if you had to carve a cache out of the base 640 KB of RAM, you gave up kilobytes grudgingly. Earlier caching programs also didn't handle very large caches as well as do today's far better versions. Now, it's not uncommon to find a cache of 2 MB or even more on a well-equipped PC. And a PC with a multi-megabyte cache absolutely *flies*.

Caching is so important to PC performance, in fact, that Microsoft includes a very good one, SMARTDRV, with Windows 3.1 and later releases. (SMARTDRV also shipped with earlier versions of Windows, but was a feeble, unworthy program in those days.) Super PC-Kwik is better than SMARTDRV, but the performance of both programs under Windows is close, so most Windows users simply use SMARTDRV.

Here are some rules of thumb on cache sizes for notebook and laptop PCs:

Recommended Disk Cache Sizes

Memory installed	If running DOS	If running *Windows*
640 KB	32 KB	NR
1 MB	128 KB	NR
2 MB	1 MB	NR
3 MB	2 MB	256 KB
4 MB	2 MB	512 KB
5 MB	NR	1 MB
6–12 MB	NR	2 MB

NR = configuration not recommended

Users of battery-powered portables get a second big gain from using a good caching program. Because it reduces the number of times the PC must access the hard disk—a battery-draining procedure—a caching utility can also markedly extend the operating life of your portable between battery charges.

All in all, disk-caching is about as close as you can get in the PC world to something for nothing. Even if you have only enough RAM installed to set aside just a small cache, you'll get a noticeable improvement in performance. With a larger cache, the results are phenomenal.

Windows users get the necessary software free in the box; and for those who eschew Windows and prefer to run their machines under DOS, the good news is that a number of portable-PC makers are now bundling copies of Super PC-Kwik with their machines.

Either way, disk-caching is one of the great bargains of computing.

Stacker

Step right up, ladies and gentlemen. Have I got an offer for you!

How would you like a new hard disk for your laptop or notebook computer—almost for free? That's right, I'm almost GIVING AWAY hard disks here. I'll match whatever size disk you have in your portable PC, and I'll even jam this new, almost-free disk right in there with your existing disk... so you'll have TWICE the capacity of your existing disk! Maybe even more!

See that little coupon down at the bottom of the page? Just fill it in and send it to me with a check for $75, and I'll send you . . . .

No, no, no. It doesn't work that way. But almost.

One of the most useful products ever for portable PC owners has emerged from the obscurity of the utility software ghetto to solve our inevitable hard disk-capacity problems. Breathes there a notebook user with a soul so dead that he has never said "HELP! I'm running out of space on my hard disk!"?

Hard disks for portable PCs have gotten bigger at a remarkable clip. The old 20 MB disk-capacity standard is thoroughly obsolete; now 60 MB and 80 MB disks are commonplace in even the smallest notebook PCs, and 120 MB and larger mini-disks are starting to appear in this tiny form factor. Laptop PCs, of course, can already accept disks with capacities several times that large.

But it's a fact of computing life—call it Seymour's third law, if you wish—that no matter how large the disk in your portable PC, before long it'll be too small. Especially with Windows (allow about 8 MB of disk space), *OS/2* (allow 31 MB), and applications such as Word for Windows, Excel, Freelance Graphics for Windows, Quattro Pro/Windows and many, many other Windows programs—which take from 5 MB to 8 or 10 MB *each*—hard disk real estate is disappearing rapidly.

Swapping your portable's existing hard disk for a new one is one answer. But it's expensive and wasteful (what are you going to do with the old disk?) and sometimes technically messy (will your dealer take care of copying over to the new disk all your files, maintaining your directory structure as he does so?).

Stacker to the rescue. It's the best of several "on-the-fly" compression utilities now available. With the release of Stacker 2.0 in the fall of 1991, Stac Electronics finally made it safe for PC users to rely on full-time on-the-fly compression.

File compression is one of the black arts of the PC business. It relies on the notion of replacing repetitive chunks of data in your file with *tokens,* or abbreviated codes, which upon decompression restore precisely the right data in precisely the right place in the file. Modern decompression technology arises from the work of two Israeli academics, Abraham Lempel and Jacob Ziv, who in 1977 published a paper on their Lempel-

Ziv Compression Algorithm. It is a complex piece of mathematics and has become the foundation of essentially every commercial compression program.

But there's more to deal with here: there are two fundamentally different kinds of file compression, both based on the Lempel-Ziv work.

The first includes such useful programs as PKZIP, which can compress specific existing files at your request, then uncompress them when you're ready to use them again. That's *offline compression.* You have to intervene to squeeze the file down, then intervene again to expand the file to its original form. Both are time-consuming steps, but they can be very useful, as when you're trying to squeeze as much fat as possible out of a file you have to send by modem, or when you need to shrink a group of files to fit on a floppy disk you're sending to someone else. Just make sure whomever receives that file knows they're getting a compressed file—and that they have the same file-compression program you have, so they can unpack the file and get to work.

By contrast, on-the-fly compression, as in Stacker, is real-time, *online compression.* It takes no intervention or selection on your part; every file your applications write to disk is automatically compressed as it's saved. And decompressed when that application opens the file again. Neither you, your application program, nor DOS can tell that compression and decompression have been applied.

Thus Stacker in effect doubles the size of your hard disk—any hard disk, on any PC—by compressing files as they're saved, then uncompressing them as they're used again. When you install Stacker, it creates a ghost drive on your PC, then packs your existing drive's data into that space and erases the original full-size files. Installation is as close to automatic and bullet-proof as possible; you don't need to know anything about Lempel-Ziv or any other arcane technological bits to put Stacker to work for you.

The exact net gain in disk space is hard to predict, because file compressibility varies by file type. Word processing files, spreadsheet files, and database files are moderately compressible—usually, by a little better than 2:1. Graphics files, especially big TIFF files as used in desktop publishing, can be compressed much more—often, by 6:1, 8:1, even 10:1. So you can't be sure until you've installed *Stacker* just how much more hard disk space you'll have. But at least twice as much space is a good bet. (Though in fact the average compression of files under Stacker is somewhat higher, the program intentionally does not compress some files, such as DOS system files, which must be available at start-up in their original form. Allowing for these uncompressed files leaves a net gain of about 100 percent in disk space.)

Stacker and other, similar on-the-fly programs exact three small prices, beyond their modest purchase cost. The first is that saving a file, and then opening it, is marginally slower than without compression and decompression. The differences are small, and given the gain in disk space they're immaterial, but they do exist.

The second cost is in memory: Stacker relies on a 40 KB device driver, called from your CONFIG.SYS file, to perform its tricks. But it's a well-behaved driver, and can almost always be tucked away up in high memory (above 640 KB), so it should make little if any difference in your available memory.

Finally, once you install Stacker, you cannot use conventional DOS or add-on utilities for such functions as defragmenting your disk. That's because Stacker adds to the gains possible with the Lempel-Ziv formulas additional savings in disk space through breaking some of DOS's most sacrosanct rules. DOS stores files in sectors and clusters of fixed size. No matter how much space is left over after DOS tucks data into a sector, and its big brother, the cluster (a group of sectors), DOS assigns that whole unit to the file. In other words, DOS mindlessly throws away a lot of space on your hard disk.

It's a little like watching a movie, where you're sitting in the dark, staring at a blank screen two thirds of the time: the projected, frame-by-frame image is visible only about one third of the time, while the persistence of vision phenomenon fools us into thinking we're seeing a continuous image.

Stacker uses its own more-efficient scalable disk-storage system; its device driver accepts commands from DOS and your applications, then translates them into Stacker's way of thinking about disk storage. If you use DOS disk-management commands, or those found in such popular packages as Central Point Software's PC Tools or Symantec's Norton Utilities, you can destroy the *Stacker* files—taking your data with them.

To avoid those problems, Stacker includes its own defragmentation and "unerase" utilities (licensed, modified version of the Norton packages' similar programs). Use the utilities provided with *Stacker* and you won't have any trouble.

I am innately skeptical of products such as on-the-fly-compression utilities, because I always fear that something will go wrong and I'll lose all my data. But Stacker is so carefully and robustly designed that I have come to trust it without reservation.

And I love the results: a second hard disk, almost for free. Maybe they *should* start running ads in the computer magazines, with little coupons . . . .

Battery Watch

Given the relatively short running time per charge-cycle of most portable PCs' batteries, it's curious and often frustrating that methods of estimating the remaining operating time of a battery are so crude. If your battery consistently delivers, say, $2^1/2$ hours of service from a fully charged state to the point when your PC starts beeping and you know it's about to shut down, then it's easy enough, if you start out with a freshly charged battery every time, to know how long you can work before the system is going to go dark.

But most of time we *don't* start out with a freshly charged battery and run it 'til it drops. Rather, we use up battery life in a series of shorter bursts: an hour here, 20 minutes there, then 15 minutes more. Thus each time we turn on the PC after that first session, it's a guessing game as to just how much operating time is really left. Especially since batteries last somewhat longer between charges when used in those short bursts, making an intelligent estimate of remaining battery life is difficult and extremely inexact.

Portable-PC makers have tried to get around this problem in several ways. Compaq has recently made progress with a built-in battery meter in its LTE Lite notebook series, but overall, judging the state of your portable's battery remains a black art.

A clever utility, Battery Watch, can make your life a lot easier. From Travelling Software, the LapLink people, Battery Watch is an easily installed pop-up utility which predicts with very good accuracy the time remaining on the battery currently installed in your notebook or laptop. Indeed, Battery Watch is so useful that some notebook PC manufacturers have burned it into a ROM chip inside their machines; others include the disk-based version as a bundle with their machines. But even if you have to buy a copy, the modest street price of the current version, Battery Watch Pro, only about $25 – $30, makes it a steal.

Right out of the box, Battery Watch "knows" about most current notebook and laptop PCs' battery-life characteristics. If its extensive list of the machines for which it has already been calibrated doesn't include your portable, it's easy enough to "train" Battery Watch about the power-consumption characteristics of your system. And the program's smart enough to know that you may have an extra battery or two; it can track them, too.

You can pop up Battery Watch's simple gas-gauge display any time you want an update on the time remaining on your battery. In my experience, with several different laptop and notebook PCs, it's accurate to within a couple of minutes—and closer than that I don't need.

The program will even handle occasional deep-discharging of your battery—draining it as close to empty as possible, so you can avoid one of the nasty habits of partly discharged nickel-cadmium batteries: losing capacity over time.

And unlike some memory-hogging terminate-and-stay-resident utilities, which seem to think using 50 KB to 100 KB of RAM is acceptable, Battery Watch Pro can be configured to take up as little as 6K of RAM.

Few utilities work so well or so transparently as Battery Watch Pro, and hardly any deliver so much value for such a low price. It's on my must-have list for portable PCs.

Laptop UltraVision

Portable-PC displays are a lot better than they used to be. The days of coarse resolution, distorted proportions, tiny displays, and dim and generally illegible notebook and laptop PC screens are nearly over. Now we have VGA resolution; pie charts instead of egg charts; screens large enough to let you see your work; and backlit screens usable in almost any light level.

What we don't have yet, unfortunately, are really readable onscreen typefaces.

Laptop UltraVision to the rescue. An offshoot of a well-established, award-winning utility program for desktop PCs, Laptop UltraVision makes much better use of an LCD screen, including using its full height. The program provides a wide variety of alternative screen fonts, which replace the squatty, unattractive characters burned into your portable's ROM chips. UltraVision's fonts use the full 640 × 480-pixel resolution of the VGA standard, not the reduced 640 × 400-pixel area most VGA-level LCD displays default to in text mode. In addition, these characters are larger, each formed in an 8 × 19-pixel box, not the 8 × 16-pixel box of most LCD screens' characters. That produces a much more open, attractive and legible character set.

In addition to those better-looking fonts, Laptop UltraVision also lets you display more lines of text onscreen if you wish—in smaller fonts, of course. You can choose a normal 25-line display, or (on a VGA display) 34-, 50- or 60-line displays. The latter two are nearly illegible to my eye, but can be useful when I want a bird's-eye view of a large spreadsheet.

While Laptop UltraVision provides a library of 22 different fonts to choose from, that's a little deceptive, because many of those fonts are ugly, gaudy things few would seriously consider using. I find UltraVision's SANS 2 font perfect for my needs; I'm sure you'll find one or two you like, too.

An unexpected advantage of using Laptop UltraVision is that text-based screen redraws are much faster. The improvement in text-display speed depends on the laptop or notebook PC on which UltraVision is running, and also on the application program in use. But the improvement is always noticeable, and sometimes spectacular: tested on five notebooks and laptops from Compaq, Toshiba and Zeos, the speed-up ranged from one-and-a-half to three times normal text-display speed. Many video utilities slow down screen redraws in return for their promised gains in image quality; Laptop UltraVision actually speeds-up the process, as well as providing more legible displays.

Windows applications don't benefit from the use of Laptop UltraVision, because Windows applications rely on graphical displays, and UltraVision affects only text display. But if you load UltraVision first, then Windows, you'll find UltraVision's superior text-handling is available to standard DOS applications run under Windows, so long as they are displayed full-screen. (Run those DOS applications in a window, of course, and you're back to Windows' much-slower display performance.)

Laptop UltraVision takes up just 16 KB of RAM, and costs in the $50 range. It's not a necessity, but it can sure make your life a lot easier; your eyes will thank you for using it.

Your Usual Apps . . . *Please!*

Elsewhere in this book I've talked about the importance of staying with Windows applications on your portable PC if you rely on Windows apps on your desktop machine, and conversely, staying with DOS apps in your portable if you're a confirmed DOS user at your desk.

The idea is simple: Don't see a notebook or laptop PC as a different beast, with different demands, requiring you to use different programs. But the division isn't nearly so simple as merely between Windows and non-Windows applications. Many software publishers, for example, are now starting to produce "junior" versions of their mainstream applications, ostensibly to meet the special needs of the laptop or notebook user.

What special needs? Today's portable PCs have big hard disks, good displays, fine keyboards, and run a lot faster than most of the desktop PCs currently in use. These half-baked, half-wit versions of programs are unnecessary relics of another era.

WordPerfect Corporation, for example, sells LetterPerfect, a smaller, simplified version of its market-leading word-processing program. The apparent rationale for this approach is twofold: the kinds of people who use notebooks and laptops probably aren't smart enough to learn to use the real thing—as their secretaries and assistants do—and so they need a special, smaller, simpler version; and, second, LetterPerfect can be run on a less powerful machine than "real" WordPerfect.

Nonsense! We don't need crippled, pint-sized versions of the software we use at our desks. This kind of thinking harks back to the days when a laptop PC barely accepted 640 KB of RAM, and had one or two floppy disk drives but no hard disk. (Just as LetterPerfect harks back to the days of WordPerfect Executive, the company's first junior-sized package, designed to run from a floppies-only laptop.)

You'll go nuts switching between two different-sized versions of the same program. Stick with what you know and rely on, and don't let anyone sell you on the idea that your notebook or laptop PC is a lame duck in need of a lightweight version of your favorite programs.

Eye Relief

OK, now I'm going to work the other side of the street for a minute. That's a delicious privilege for an author; bear with me for a minute and you'll see why I'm changing my tune this one time.

I just argued that you should stay with all your favorite programs on your laptop or notebook PC, and not fall victim to the fallacy that portable PCs have some strange force-field around them which requires you to buy special, diminished versions of programs for them. And now I'm going to argue that there's an exception to that rule, one special application program that you should use on your laptop or notebook, even though it duplicates the functions of a category of program you almost certainly already own, use, and know well: your word processor.

The exception that proves my rule here is Eye Relief, a brilliant little word-processing program from Ken Skier, proprietor of Lexington, Massachusetts' SkiSoft. It was developed specifically for portable PCs—though many of us who rely on it have come to like it so much that we also have a copy on our desktop machines.

Eye Relief's premise is simple: you need bigger, easier-to-read type onscreen when you're writing something on a portable PC. Not just a little bigger, as with Laptop UltraVision's slightly larger and better-formed characters. I mean HUGEly bigger, giant characters so easy to read that you'll never squint at your screen again.

Oh, yes: Ken believes notebook PC word processors should be *fast.* Eye Relief is entirely RAM-resident, and I'm confident in saying that you'll never find a faster text editor. Of course, another advantage of a RAM-resident word processor—and especially of one which keeps its data files entirely in RAM, too—is that it lengthens battery life significantly, since the program isn't always running out to the computer's hard disk for some more code or data. You can probably also turn down the backlighting on your notebook or laptop's display—and backlighting is the single biggest consumer of battery power on your machine. Score one more for Eye Relief.

Eye Relief's onscreen typeface is about as plain as can be, a rough copy of the monospaced Courier typeface IBM made famous on millions of Selectric typewriters. But in its four text sizes—Skier calls them tiny, small, medium, and large; I'd call them normal, large, very large, and *huge*—it reads perfectly onscreen. The "tiny" size is only slightly, and unimportantly, larger than the type in the usual 80-character-line screen display. "Small" is useful for me when I want to see a whole block of work—say, a paragraph, plus the end of the preceding paragraph and the beginning of the following one. I usually write in the "Medium" setting, which provides about 30 characters per line. And when my eyes are really tired, I sometimes, but only rarely, kick Eye Relief into its "large" setting, which shows only 9 lines of about 22 characters each onscreen, but can be read from across the room.

Indeed, the extraordinary legibility of Eye Relief displays in the two largest type sizes leads to the program's only potential liability: people sitting around you can easily read the screen. That may not matter much when you're sitting alone, at your desk, in your den, or at a desk in your hotel room; but it might matter a great deal when you're working in seat 533E on a 747, and the six people sitting nearest you are reading over your shoulder. One of the pleasures of Eye Relief's good program design is that you can instantly flip from one text-size setting to another with hot keys, so it's perfectly possible to work at the "tiny" type setting, then quickly flip to the larger characters of the program's "small" or "medium" settings, check a passage, then flip back into its nearly normal "tiny" type.

Another unexpected advantage of those highly legible large type sizes is that you can, in a pinch, use your notebook PC as a kind of electronic cue card when giving a hurried presentation. A few times I've written, or rewritten, a speech at the last minute; then rather than printing it out (usually, because I didn't have available a printer with large type), just propped the notebook up on the lectern and spoke using my notes displayed on the PC's screen under Eye Relief, as a poor man's Teleprompter.

The formatting and printing tools in Eye Relief are, well, primitive. Skier's notion is that people should use Eye Relief to get their text into the computer and in final, edited form, then read the Eye Relief file into their favorite word processor for fancying-up and printing. Happily, Eye Relief saves text in plain ASCII files, which can be imported effortlessly into everything from WordPerfect and Microsoft Word to Word for Windows, XyWrite, even 1-2-3.

Is that limited formatting and printing a problem for you? Remember, this isn't a program for fancy paper output, but for *getting text down fast,* even when it's 11 P.M., you've been working since 7 this morning, you're sitting there at 35,000 feet squeezed into a coach class seat between two Olympic weight-lifters, rubbing your eyes and wondering how much longer it will be before you can just get some sleep . . . .

While formatting and printing controls may be minimal, there's nothing crude about Eye Relief's capabilities as a text editor. It allows you to choose from many combinations of foreground (text) and background colors (which is even more important when you're working with monochrome LCD screens' peculiar translations of colors). It has all the usual search and replace tools. It lets you write, store, and execute macros.

There are nice, up-to-date drop-down menus, which can be called from function keys or from a moving-cursor bar, with plenty of quick, obvious keyboard shortcuts (such as CTRL-P to print, CTRL-Q to quit, etc.) Looking for sophistication in program design? Eye Relief even allows you to minutely vary the spacing between characters onscreen, so very large type sizes don't look wonky, with so much space between them that they become harder, not easier, to read.

Finally, do you want to know how many words you've written? Just hit CTRL-W, and Eye Relief will give you an instant word count. (OK, I admit that this is a bigger deal for writers, especially columnists, who must frequently write to a specific length, than for most people.)

Problems? I've never found any. The manual is spare, a few pages of large-type printout (to make it easy to read for the vision-impaired, who love the program). But that's not a criticism; Eye Relief is so easy to use that I used the program for six months before I opened the manual . . . and then I grabbed it only to find SkiSoft's number to buy another copy of the program.

I've come to like Eye Relief so much that I often use it on desktop PCs, especially when I want to force myself to concentrate entirely on *what* I'm writing, not on how it's going to look when I'm finished. And I simply won't use a notebook or laptop PC without it.

All this convenience costs just $129 list, less than $100 from one of the relatively few dealers which stock the program. Listen; try this one, you'll like it. You'll love it. And I'll bet your letters, proposals, reports, whatever you write, read better, too, because Eye Relief forces you to focus on *what you want to say,* not on how you want it to look.

Hot Line

One of the slickest things about travelling with a laptop or notebook PC is that you can carry your Rolodex, personal phone book, or other directory-style contacts-file information with you. If, that is, you go to the effort of putting it into the computer in the first place.

I've long raved about Hot Line 2, the best name-and-address-file and autodialing program in existence. It's a DOS pop-up program, which also runs fine full-screen or in a window under Windows. Easy to set up and even easier to use, Hot Line saves me an hour a day when I'm working at my desk. But it's even more important when I'm travelling: when I'm in the office and can't find a name or number, there's always someone who can track it down for me. How am I supposed to do that when I'm in a hotel room in San Jose . . . ?

I don't usually use Hot Line's auto-dialer capabilities when I'm travelling. It's not worth hooking up the notebook PC's modem to the hotel phone line just to dial phone numbers automatically. Even if I'm already connected to a hotel phone system for sending data messages and maybe faxes, too, I still don't auto-dial voice calls; there are too many complications with the different prefixes required by different hotel phone systems.

But auto-dialing isn't what's important: what *is* important is that I have my complete desktop file of 3,900-plus names, addresses, phone numbers, fax numbers, etc., with me as I travel.

Sometimes, of course, it's not very convenient to look up a name or number in a computerized phone list. For those occasions, I also carry a small, booklet-sized printout, which lists just the names and phone numbers from my Hot Line contacts file. Printed with Books, Cards and Labels, an odd little utility which handles front-and-back (book-style) printing from database files, it's a great convenience when I don't have the time or patience to open my notebook PC, turn it on and load Hot Line.

The real advantage comes from having created that computerized file in the first place. We use the same Hot Line data file—mercifully, a standard dBASE .DBF file—on every PC in my office, so everyone has access to that pool of information. And so we all have the same, current version of the data.

And thanks to Hot Line, I can have it at my fingertips, no matter where in the world I may be.

Hot Line isn't a laptop or notebook program; there's nothing in Hot Line specific to portable computers. But keeping up with names, addresses, and telephone numbers is an absolutely fundamental application in business, and Hot Line is the best tool I've found for the job.

That it works so well on portable PCs is pure gravy.

II.

HITTING THE ROAD

Travelling with a Notebook

Ever read John Steinbeck's "Travels With Charley"? It recounts a leisurely trip Steinbeck made in the company of his dog. Charley is a good and faithful companion, and while you won't get nearly so many laughs out of your notebook or laptop PC on your own wanderings as Steinbeck did from Charley, there are parallels.

Unless you want to wear your notebook like a watch fob from a college honorary society—just to prove how cool you are—you want it to earn its keep on the road. Which means keeping it working and keeping it busy.

Here's a long list of ways you can stay out of trouble and turn that portable computer into a real productivity tool, not a seven-pound albatross, when you travel.

Dealing with the Airlines

I still run into people who worry that the airlines may not let them board with a portable PC—or if they'll let them onboard, that they won't let them use the PC, once aloft. That hasn't been the case for a long time, though I do concede that there was a time when there was a lot of confusion about the idea of using PCs onboard commercial aircraft, and most of the airlines made a mess of explaining their often-conflicting positions.

Today, there are no restrictions on any U.S.-flag carriers on the use of PCs in flight—and none that I've been able to find among the foreign-flag carriers, either. That's not to say that there isn't a small national airline somewhere that hasn't yet caught on, but I'd be very surprised if any of the readers of this book ever get hassled by airline personnel about using their computers in the air.

(If you do, please write me a note, in care of Brady Books, and I'll look into the situation for the next edition of this book.)

I should say that getting through security is another matter altogether. There's a lot more on this in "X-Ray Machines and Airline Security," later in this section, but if you're flying on a beleaguered airline (El Al, for example) or into or out of a beleaguered nation (again, El Al's service into and out of Israel) or on an extremely security-conscious airline (SwissAir is the prime example), you're likely to get questioned a few times about *anything* electronic in your baggage.

Patience, patience. Remember, they're trying to save your life.

Beyond Tray Tables: Computing in the Air

Though there may be few legal hassles with using your PC onboard commercial aircraft these days, there are plenty of other little problems waiting for you onboard.

A thought for travelling PC users: while you're complaining about the various inconveniences and compromises of working in the air, consider that your own behavior might be a source of annoyance to your fellow travellers. Most of the problems I see in the air arise from just this kind of human failing—people with little consideration for their seatmates and others around them, people who drop computers on your head when they try to retrieve them from overhead baggage compartments, people who persist in working noisily at 3:45 A.M. when you're trying desperately to get another two hours' sleep before you land in Bangkok and have to race to a meeting.

So give some thought to your own behavior when you pop open your PC on airlines. There is an airborne-computing code of etiquette, even if it's an unwritten code.

For a start, please be careful if you have to dig your PC out of a case stuffed into the overhead bins. Twice I've been hit on the head by notebook PCs dropped by people as they were grubbing around in overhead baggage compartments. I acknowledge that my preference for aisle seats makes this slightly more likely than if I sat over against the window, but I don't think choosing an aisle seat should be an invitation to get my head bashed in. I wasn't badly hurt either time, but I had fierce headaches afterwards. One clown who dropped a Compaq SLT 286 on my head—not your basic lightweight machine, please note—followed up by a few minutes later by braining me with a spare battery dropped from that same attache case in the overhead, leaving a deep cut.

I've seen other passengers clipped by PCs dropped accidentally from overstuffed bags in overstuffed baggage bins, and I've seen several more laptops and notebooks fall right to the floor, without hitting anyone but with disastrous results for the machines.

I spend a lot of time in the air, so I've probably seen this happen more than you have. Trust me: it's a real problem. Don't bash up the guy sitting next to you or across the aisle from you when you reach for your PC. He may not be as forgiving as I am, and you may wind up with a lawsuit on your hands.

It's better by far—it's both more convenient and also safer—to slip your PC carrying case under the seat in front of you. That's especially true when you have an inboard seat, and would have to stand up and push past your seatmates to get to the aisle, so you could reach the overhead bin.

Be considerate, as well, when passengers around you are going through the rituals of airline travel. During meal service, for example, you might fold up your PC and put it away. Especially if you're sitting in the aisle in a three-abreast row of seats, it's pretty tough for a flight attendant to reach over your machine to pass trays of food to the people between you and the window. Take a break, have your dinner (or not, if you dislike airline food as much as I do), then go back to work.

Note that there's an element of self-preservation here, too: I've watched attendants spill coffee, wine, and dirty flatware onto people's PCs. A falling table knife could easily shatter an LCD display, and I'm highly confident that the coffee and wine I've seen poured into people's keyboards didn't do those machines any good. (The damage from keyboard spills—a common-enough hazard on *terra firma*—is rarely immediately evident: you don't see sparks or hear loud noises. You just wake up one nice morning a few days or weeks later to find your PC isn't working any more . . . and you wonder why.)

Finally, think twice before pounding away on your machine through the night on red-eye flights. I'm a two-finger typist, which means my "keyboarding" sounds something like artillery softening up an enemy's beaches before a major amphibious landing. I've learned to type more discreetly and quietly when I must—as on airplanes, for example—and I confess that I sometimes do work through the night on red-eyes. But I try to be very quiet—no triumphant *bang!* on the Enter key at the end of difficult paragraphs!—and I try hard to do that late-night work only when I must.

I suggest that you try the quiet-typing trick, too, when you must work—and think, especially on long night-time flights, about just how much you really "must" get that work done right then.

Comfort and convenience are important, too.

For example, I almost never work on the little fold-down or pull-up tables built into airliners. On a few long overseas flights, in business class and first class, the tables which come up out of your armrest aren't too bad. But the little devils that fold down from the back of the seat in front are disasters. They're almost never deep enough; they're wobbly and unsteady; and then the guy in front of you decides to lean back for a snooze, and as he rams his seat back into your knees, be breaks the display off your open notebook PC.

Instead, I ask the flight attendant for two or three of those little pillows the airlines hand out, and two or three blankets. I cross my legs and build a sort of platform in my lap, with the pillows on the bottom and the blankets, still folded, on top. I can push and squeeze and generally contort this squishy pile into a wonderful little impromptu desk. The PC snuggles neatly and securely into this pile of fabric and padding, where it's much more comfortable to see and use.

This has the added advantage of making the machine much quieter to use, too, since you don't have a plastic tray beneath the PC as a sound-reflecting panel.

It takes me a minute or two longer to get untangled from this cocoon when the person next to me decides to make a trip to the lavatory, but the incredible comfort it brings is well worth the trouble.

My last thought on comfort, good manners, and good working habits on airlines is to be sensitive to what the person sitting next to you might be reading on the screen of your PC. Though most LCD displays have pretty narrow viewing angles, with the result that someone next to you would usually have a hard time seeing what you're working on, I often see people peering over or around newspaper and magazines at the screens on their neighbors' PCs, desperately trying to read the information.

Often enough, they can make it out.

During the height of the takeover craze in the late '80s, I sat next to two financial analysts from a large Wall Street investment banking house who were working together on a laptop PC on plans for what turned out to be a big, splashy, controversial takeover offer. They were pulling together the numbers for the offer, and were using the PC to outline their "action plan." At least two of us sitting nearby were merrily reading the information off their screen, winking at each other as we marvelled at their indiscretion.

Yes, we were bad boys, and should have just looked the other way. Yes, we were being rude. But they were fools to make it so easy for us.

X-Ray Machines and Airline Security

It's a common misconception that PCs and magnetic media will be damaged by putting them through airport x-ray security systems. Nothing about x-rays is known to be harmful to either PCs or disks, so you can relax on that count.

But there's more to the story than x-ray damage.

The real risk to the hard disk in your laptop or notebook PC, and to any floppy disks you may be carrying, lies in the powerful AC transformer inside the x-ray system's cabinet. Power transformers throw off powerful magnetic fields, and depending on where the transformer is in that x-ray machine and how your bag lands on the conveyor belt, your disks could be affected by the transformer's magnetic field. It takes an exceptionally powerful magnetic field to fully erase a disk, so that's unlikely. More likely, by far, is a partial loss of data, from already-weak places on the disk, where the level of coercivity, or magnetic force, required to lose a few bits may be much lower.

So while x-rays themselves won't damage your computer, putting your computer equipment through an airport x-ray machine isn't a very good idea. I never put mine on the conveyor belt if I can avoid it; instead, I ask for a hand inspection.

In the U.S., airport security people are required to hand-inspect baggage at the owners' request, though you may occasionally find an uncooperative security person who grumbles about the extra work.

Abroad, customs and laws vary, but in many parts of the Middle East and especially in Switzerland, be prepared to run the machine through the x-ray tunnel and hope for the best: you're not likely to get very far with hand-inspection requests.

Whether you run your PC through the x-ray tunnel or not, be prepared for requests to take it out, set it up and turn it on. This is reasonable, and though it's often a nuisance—especially if you're running for a tight connection—you'll regret it if you tell the security people that's just not necessary. Remember the old policeman's line, "You may beat the rap, but you can't beat the ride"? In other words, "A smart lawyer may get you off, but son, you are *mine* for an hour or two if I decide to take you downtown and book you"?

Something like that applies with airport security people, too. Give them unwarranted grief and they'll give you . . . unwarranted grief.

The point of turning the PC on, of course, is to make sure it's not a bomb in disguise. Portable computers look especially fearsome viewed through an airport x-ray scanner. They're small, flat, have a maze of wires inside, and then, off to one side, there's this suspicious, opaque thing you and I know to be a battery. But which could just as easily be a wad of plastic explosive. All those other wires? The timing and trigger mechanisms, of course.

The moral here is simple: be prepared. Don't travel by air with a notebook or laptop PC whose battery is fully discharged, if you can help it. Do you really want to have to dig out your AC power supply brick and go through the charade of finding an outlet, plugging things in, turning the PC on? Then repacking everything?

And if your PC's battery *is* exhausted, and the system won't boot, make *very* sure the AC brick isn't stashed in that suitcase you checked five minutes ago . . . .

Dogtags for Your PC

It's amazing how many notebook and laptop PCs stray from their owners' hands. In an earlier book, *Jim Seymour's PC Productivity Bible,* I recounted how I'd managed to lose, or have stolen, laptop PCs I'd travelled with, and how I got them back; and I offered some suggestions on how to make sure the people who eventually find your machine can get it back to you.

I was amazed at the reader mail that followed: dozens and dozens of stories from others who'd lost their PCs, but had the good fortune to get them back in good condition. Sure, if a thief steals your PC, you're not likely to see it again. But if it's simply forgotten somewhere or misplaced—and sometimes, even if it *has* been stolen by a miscreant—there are steps you can take now that may improve your chances of getting it back.

The first line of defense is obvious: Put your name on your notebook or laptop. When I get a new portable PC, one of the first things I do is tape a couple of business cards onto it. There's always one on the bottom, and there's usually one on the top of the lid, as well. If the machine has its own case, I scatter business cards throughout the pockets of that case, as well—and put one in the little clear-plastic-faced pocket many of these cases provide explicitly for that purpose.

It's important to tape cards onto portables in a way that will defend against the rigors of travel. You want a single, wide piece of clear tape covering the entire card, and reaching out at least a half inch all around. If you don't have any wide Scotch tape in your department, check with your company's shipping department: they probably have tough, wide, clear tape for covering shipping labels. If that doesn't work, try your local office stationer, or even better, call Highsmith, the library-supplies company, for a roll of their thick, clear, incredibly tough four-inch-wide book tape: it's the best answer of all.

The second line of defense is a sign-on message in your AUTOEXEC.BAT file asking for return of the computer, giving your name and phone number, and offering a reward for its return to you. That should be followed by a PAUSE line in the AUTOEXEC, to make sure a stranger booting up the machine can't miss the message. My onscreen message reads like this:

```
REM
REM      If this computer is found, please call
REM    one of the numbers below for return info,
REM    and details on a REWARD for its return:
REM
REM        (427) 555-5529 (office, 9-5, M-F)
REM        (427) 555-6612 (home, anytime)
REM
REM    Thank You!
REM                          —Jim Seymour
REM
PAUSE
```

It's easy to create that message. Just use your favorite word processor to open your AUTOEXEC.BAT file, add those lines near the beginning, and then save the file in plain ASCII form (*i.e.,* unformatted) under the same name.

The next time your PC boots up, it will display the message and wait for someone to hit a key before continuing. The PAUSE line at the end causes DOS to add the `Strike any key when ready . . .` prompt.

(Note that I included only phone numbers in my "please return" message—no home address. Providing your address is an invitation to a thief who might steal the computer to come check out all the *other* nifty electronics—and valuables—you have at home. An office address would be fine, but is unnecessary; someone finding your PC is going to call the phone numbers first, and you can then give them the address to which the machine should be sent.)

I mentioned the pile of skeptical—nay, cynical—reader mail I got when I suggested in print that these steps might help bring an errant PC home.

Let me give you two examples from my own experience about how they can work. In one case, I left a Toshiba T3100 portable in the overhead-luggage bin of a flight into Chicago. I hurried off the plane to make a tight connection to the West Coast—and left the computer behind. Airline people found the PC, and when they brought it out the jetway to the gate area, a helpful, computer-savvy passenger turned it on to see what would happen. The "please return" message flashed on; airline people called my office and were told where I was headed; the computer was put on the next flight to my final destination. I had it back in my hands in hours.

In a second episode, a portable was stolen from my hotel room in northern California. The thieves, or their fence, brought it into a Bay Area PC store to try to sell it. The store clerk told them to leave it so he could check it over, and come back later. When he turned it on, the message came up, and he called the police, as well as my office. Unfortunately they never nabbed the bad guys—they didn't come back—but I had the computer back, unharmed, in a couple of days.

There are lots of good people out there who'd like to help you get your things back, whether you lose them or they're stolen. Make it easy for them and they'll make you proud. Adding this kind of electronic backup in the machine itself, and just taping your business card to the outside of your notebook or laptop, is like putting dogtags on the machine—they'll help a friendly stranger send it home.

Travelling 'Cheat Sheets'

I'm a big fan of cheat sheets. Not for your teenager during math tests, but for you, when you're travelling with your portable PC far from your office and its shelf full of manuals.

For years I've carried a small, crummy-looking cheat sheet in the same case with my portable PC. Actually, it hasn't been the *same* sheet throughout that time, because I update it frequently. It includes an amazing miscellany of information. Some is obvious and typical of the notes carried by many business travellers: 800 numbers for the airline, car rental, and hotel outfits I use; a few more key phone numbers, such as for my doctor, our pediatrician, a couple of neighbors, and family members; fax numbers for a handful of clients and friends; and some personal stuff such as blood-type and a list of the medication I'm taking.

A lot more interesting are the arcane items related to using my computer and software: 800 telephone numbers for the online and e-mail services I use, for example, plus a list of keyboard shortcuts for Windows (in case I lose the mouse I carry); the more-obscure commands I rarely use for the five or six programs on which I rely; 800 numbers for support from the vendors of those programs; 800 support numbers for vendors of the hardware I carry (or am likely to encounter and borrow or be forced to use) when I'm travelling; the day, night, and fax numbers for two computer-repair services I use; account names and passwords for my e-mail accounts and the 800 numbers for customer support at those services; and more.

I strongly recommend that you make up a similar cheat sheet and stick it in your portable computer's case or other traveling bag.

Protect the surface so that the constant rubbing back-and-forth of the bag's fabric doesn't wear away the type—especially if, like me, you do your cheat sheet in small type on a laser printer, the output of which is particularly vulnerable to abrasion. I trim mine to 4 x 5 inches, slip it into an old 4x5 color transparency sleeve, then tape the ends shut. I want to protect it, but not *glorify* it—say, by laminating it—because I don't want any disincentives to throwing it out and creating a new, updated one fairly frequently. Mine gets replaced about twice a year, and if I made it any fancier, or more permanent, I probably wouldn't update it that often.

By the way, I also make a plain-ASCII text file of the PageMaker document I use to create these cheat sheets, then copy that file itself onto the hard disk of my PC. That way, even if I can't find the cheat sheet itself, I have an electronic surrogate that I can open and read under Windows' Notepad or *Write,* or any word processor, or even by using DOS's TYPE command.

Cheat sheets aren't useful just on the road, of course; I have a similar one tucked under the keyboard of the PC I use at my desk. It skips most of the personal stuff, but has even more on obscure commands in the programs I use.

In your office, if you can't remember something about a program, it's usually easy enough to look around on a bookshelf or in your credenza, or maybe under your desk, and find the manual with the answer. Or to call a know-it-all colleague. At 30,000 feet, or at 11 P.M. in a hotel in Riyadh, that can be tough . . . .

A Stationery Portfolio

Tucked away in a dark corner of my portable computer's case is a manila file folder that makes my life a lot easier when I'm travelling.

Stashed in that folder are a couple of dozen sheets of letterhead paper, maybe twice that many matching blank sheets, and a dozen or so envelopes. There's also a small wad of first-class stamps, and a separate wad of those odd-value stamps needed for letters that weigh a little more than an ounce. And there are a few of the personalized post cards I use for quick replies to reader mail, plus some personal cards and envelopes for short notes to friends and clients.

My folder also includes a half-dozen or so Federal Express and DHL overnight-courier waybills preprinted with my company's name, address, and account number, a few clear-plastic pouches for the waybills, a couple of those big, thin overnight-courier shipping envelopes, some half-page and full-page fax cover-sheet forms from my company, and a few of our expense-account forms.

If you travel with a PC—and especially, if you sometimes carry a portable printer, as well—I think you'll find a similar cache of your most-used paper and paper forms, convenient.

Especially when I'm travelling with a portable PC for several days or more, I need to in effect carry my office on my back. Or at least, in my PC's case. I can make do with electronic mail for a lot of my work, but some still requires the formality of traditional paper output. And because I rely heavily on the overnight courier services when I travel, I want to make sending things by courier as quick and easy as possible.

Don't go overboard here—you don't need a hundred sheets of letterhead paper, a big roll of stamps, and enough FedEx supplies to send everything you own back to the office via courier. But consider making up a travelling stationery portfolio like this. It adds perhaps six ounces to my case, saves hours of time tracking things down, and helps me keep my act together when I'm on the road.

Hot-Shot Backups

Backing up the hard disk in your laptop or notebook PC presents special problems—or at least, requires some thought and planning. Those issues are dealt with at length in "Backing Up," in "At Your Desk," later in this book. Most us do our backing up in the office, so I put the material in that section. But I want to suggest a another, very different *ad hoc*kind of backups that can spare you a lot of grief when you travel.

I call these "hot-shot" backups, because they're far from complete backups, and when you get used to the idea, you'll find you make them frequently, sometimes even as a break from your work on your PC as you travel.

The idea is simple: make limited, quick backups of a few important files when you have a chance.

I often keep a hot-shot backups floppy disk tucked into the most accessible pocket of whatever case I'm using to carry my notebook PC. As I'm working, I stop occasionally—sometimes a couple of times a day; sometimes just once, in the evening; but almost always every day—and make a quick copy to that floppy disk of the files I've worked with and changed *that day*. There are rarely very many of them, and I hardly ever have any problem remembering which ones to back up. (Indeed, if I can't remember which ones I've changed, then it's been too long since I made my last hot-shot backup.)

I don't use a conventional backup program for this task, for two reasons. First, because it would be too slow and clumsy: backup software is geared to full-disk backups, or at least, to incremental backups based on file dates. My hot-shot backups are incremental, but the increment is much smaller and very often more selective than backup programs care about.

And second, because I don't want to deal with the complexities of the backup software's file-compression and formatting issues. What I want are plain, ordinary DOS copies of those files, on a disk I can stick into virtually any PC and go to work.

The easiest way to make these copies is to use DOS's XCOPY command. Introduced with MS-DOS 3.1, it's one of the most useful additions to DOS's set of "internal" commands, and for all practical purposes renders the simpler and far more crude COPY command obsolete. The key to using XCOPY is the "switches," or modifiers, you can add to the DOS command line when using it. For example, add `/S` and it will copy all the subdirectories nested under a directory named in the command (*i.e.,* `XCOPY C:\WORD\STUFF A:\WORDXTRA\STUFFBAK`).

For hot-shot backups, XCOPY's biggest advantage lies in its ability to group files to be copied. For example, if all the files you want to back up are in the directory C:\WORDS, but there are other files in that directory which you do *not* want to copy, XCOPY will accept this command, which uses the `/P`, or "Pause," switch to stop after listing the name of every file in that directory to ask if that's one you want to copy:

```
XCOPY C:\REPORT\*.* A: /P
```

Type `Y` when DOS asks if that's a file you want to copy and the copy is made; type `N` and DOS moves on to the next file in the directory.

If you're really regular about making hot-shot backups every day when you travel, you can use XCOPY's `/D` "Date" switch to copy to your hot-shot floppy only the files created *on or after a specified date.* For example,

```
XCOPY C:\REPORT\*.* A: /D:11-13-92
```

will copy every file in the subdirectory REPORT on drive C that was created on or after November 13, 1992, to the floppy disk in drive A.

Some of this could be done with COPY, but its limitations soon get frustrating; and all of it could be done with DOS's BACKUP command, but you'd get a floppy with files that couldn't be read and used as is, but only by DOS's RESTORE command. XCOPY is the tool to use.

With these hot-shot backups I'm trying to save myself from the possibility of a destructive hard-disk failure while I'm travelling. You can never be absolutely sure you've protected yourself, but with a very recent backup of just the most important files I've worked with that day, I have pretty good protection. I can always go out and buy a copy of Word, or Excel, or 1-2-3, or whatever application I need to *use* those files. What I can't do is recreate the files themselves—at least, not without a great deal of time, agony and worry.

If you read "Do You Really Want a Floppy Drive?" in "Types of Users, Types of Needs," earlier in this book, you may think I've changed my mind, or am trying to work both sides of the street. Far from it: I still think built-in floppy drives are a mistake in light, small notebook PCs. Remember that I wasn't opposed to floppy drives for notebooks, only to the size and weight penalties exacted by building them into the machines themselves.

I can stick a separate floppy drive, such as the compact units from Toshiba and NEC, into my travelling bag and make these hot-shot backups at night, in a hotel room, or maybe on a long flight, without toting that drive's extra bulk and weight around with me all day.

Truth time: I don't always make hot-shot backups. Sometimes I forget; sometimes I get lazy; sometimes I leave the separate floppy drive behind at the office when I'm carrying a floppyless PC with me. But when I can, I follow this routine, and I strongly recommend it for the peace of mind it can bring.

It's cheap insurance, at small cost in time, convenience, and supplies. And come the day you *need* that hot-shot backup. . . .

When It Breaks

No matter how wisely you buy, and how careful you are with your portable PC when you travel, there's a chance you'll wake up some nice morning in Tampa and find your computer is dead. All that data you loaded onto the machine before you left Houston is still sitting there inside the computer, of course; you just can't get at it.

What to do?

An effective emergency-repairs strategy has two phases. The first can only be addressed before you buy the machine. The second is a matter of having the right phone numbers and other information at your fingertips.

Before you buy a portable PC, consider carefully how you'll get it fixed in a hurry, especially if you're away from your usual turf. Computer makers generally have not given much thought to the needs of the travelling PC user—which is odd, since those needs are markedly different from the repair needs of someone who's always going to be using his PC at his desk. Many of the support mechanisms in place for desktop PCs—whether bought from local retailers or from direct-sales outfits—just don't map very well to the traveller's needs.

If you're on the road, and your portable PC breaks, you're going to have two priorities: getting a working machine in your hands fast, and getting at the programs and data on the hard disk in your broken machine. Shipping the PC back to its maker, for example, even for overnight exchange, just isn't very useful. You're without a machine for too long, and all your data—the critical stuff you need to make your trip a success—is off somewhere in the PC vendor's shop, on the hard disk in your broken PC.

What good is this replacement machine, when your programs and data are on the *other* one?

Among makers of portable PCs, Dell and CompuAdd provide two good examples of support strategies geared to the needs of portable computer users. Dell uses a revised version of the standard, next-day deskside-service support that's bundled into the price of most of its machines. If your Dell laptop or notebook fails when you're on the road, the first step is to call Dell's support number for help. The technician on the phone will try to get the machine up and running, if possible. But this isn't the usual tech support call, when you're sitting at your desk in front of a conventional PC. Tricks such as opening the computer's case and wriggling boards and RAM chips don't work with notebook PCs: the *last* thing that tech wants is for you to try to get into the machine's innards.

If their technician can't get you back in business, Dell sends a repairman to your hotel the next morning. Unlike the usual next-day service call, however, in which the repair person shows up with a parts kit shipped overnight by the computer maker, this repairman shows up with a brand-new Dell PC, of the same model and configuration as yours. That replacement unit is yours to use while your machine is tied up.

But remember: the problem isn't just getting a working computer, but getting at the data on *your* machine's hard disk.

So that same Xerox technician carries along a copy of a Dell program, LifeLine. If your computer can be booted at all—and the technician will work hard to get it going—LifeLine will automatically copy over everything on your machine's hard disk to the disk on the new unit. Dell says their experience has been that about 70 percent of the time, the field-service technician can recover all your data and move it to the new machine.

Your PC then goes back to the Dell factory to be fixed, and will be returned to you, its data intact, in a few days.

What if the Xerox tech can't transfer your data, because he can't get your portable running, or finds the hard disk damaged? He ships it back to Dell's headquarters in Austin, where they'll try every data-recovery trick in the book. Dell says they have an almost 100 percent success rate at recovering customer data in their labs. When the data is restored and the machine is working properly again, it's sent back to you, and you return the loaner machine—please remember to erase your data files first!—in the same packing used to send you the repaired unit.

The cost for all this? Zip; it's included in the purchase price. And after the first year, you can extend that service contract, under the same terms, for a nominal sum.

CompuAdd, another major PC direct-marketer, has what is in some ways an even more interesting and helpful program—if your CompuAdd portable breaks while you're in one of the hundred or so cities where CompuAdd has a store. Just bring your broken machine to the local CompuAdd outlet, and they'll exchange it on the spot for a brand-new, identical machine. They'll also help you transfer your programs and data from the old to the new machine.

Clearly, this is an even better deal than Dell's—if you're lucky enough (or actually, *unlucky* enough) for your PC to break when you're in the right city.

Both of these service programs show serious attention to the portable PC user's two biggest concerns when confronting a broken computer: getting back into action as quickly as possible and getting at the programs and data stored on the broken machine's hard disk.

Some other vendors have special service and support programs for portable PC users. Toshiba, for example, has an "Exceptional Care" package, under which they offer expedited repair service, and maybe a loaner in the meantime. But no other vendor I've found goes to such lengths as Dell and CompuAdd in responding to the needs of travelling computer user.

So phase one of solving repair problems begins when you choose a vendor. The importance of support on the road is so great for portable PC users that the level and quality of a vendor's support plays a large part in my choice of a portable PC supplier.

Phase two involves having what you need with you when things go wrong. This includes a piece of paper with the vendor's telephone support number, fax-line support number, and the invoice number from your purchase of the machine. (You may need that number to help the PC maker identify the specifics of your machine.) It isn't a bad idea to write the PC's serial number on that card, too. And you should list any internal components you've added to the machine since the initial purchase, such as more memory or an internal modem. That sheet should also have printouts of your current AUTOEXEC.BAT and CONFIG.SYS files. And the version of DOS you have installed on the machine.

You'll need that data when you call the PC's maker for help, and you obviously won't be able to turn on the PC to get it.

This applies principally to owners of PCs bought from direct-market vendors, of course. If your machine was sold by a computer dealer, you should also have that dealer's name, address, and telephone number, and, if at all possible, the name of someone at that shop with whom you've dealt and who has some vested interest in keeping you happy. It wouldn't hurt to have the computer maker's name, address and telephone number, too, because—sorry—you probably aren't going to get meaningful help from the dealer.

(Depending on the maker, you may not get much help from them, either, of course. Don't expect IBM or Compaq, for example, to get you up and running; they leave that to their dealers, which means that at least when you're travelling, you're probably in deep water if something goes wrong. But a desperate call to the computer maker's customer support office can often get you the name and telephone number of a recommended, authorized repair outfit in the city you're visiting.)

You should also, if at all possible, have with you floppy-disk copies of the most important programs and data on your hard disk. This needn't be a two-foot-tall stack of floppies; be ruthless about excluding everything but the most critical programs and files.

Finally, resist at all costs the temptation to get out your Swiss Army knife and go to work on the machine. The chances that you'll succeed are very small, and the innards of most notebook and many laptop PCs are so tightly packed that you'll have a devil of a time just getting the still-broken machine back together again after your failed surgery.

The Toolkit: What to Take

One of the pleasures of a modern notebook or laptop PC is its small size for the extraordinary power and convenience it brings. Unfortunately, it's all too easy to double or triple the weight of a compact, convenient notebook PC by dragging along an attache case full of accessories.

Still, there ARE some things you have to have along to get the most out of your machine: the famous irreducible minimum. Here's how to figure out what constitutes the minimum for your work style.

Floppies . . . Despite Your Hard Disk

Hard disks are such integral parts of portable computers today that it's easy to forget about those days when we routinely carried along a fistful of floppies when we travelled. Some held programs, some had data, and some were blanks, so we could do *more* work. We couldn't leave them behind: they were our only form of storage.

These days, most PC users, including laptop and notebook owners, see floppies primarily as a means of loading new software onto their machines. Shuffle those disks in and out of the machine, then put 'em in a drawer somewhere. Curiously, that's just why floppy disks were invented. IBM came up with the first 8-inch floppy disks two decades ago, as an inexpensive way of distributing software. Floppies were seen not as a useful means of data storage, but only as a good, cheap way to ship updated program code to customers.

Falling back to that view is a mistake for the travelling laptop or notebook user. I'm certainly not suggesting that you carry your programs and data on floppies, run them from the floppies and ignore the hard disk in your machine; I am suggesting that you'll find a lot of uses for a couple of blank, formatted 3½-inch floppies tucked away somewhere in your computer case.

For making hot-shot backups, for example, as described elsewhere in this book. For giving copies of your data files to others with whom you may be working—real, working copies, not dead printouts that can't be revised or recalc'ed. For sending files back to your office. For quick and easy copying of files from the hard disks on *others'* PCs to your own. For . . . lots of little jobs.

A couple of blank $3^1/_2$-inch floppy disks add about an ounce and a half to your case. You'll never notice the weight. Get a couple out of that slush pile where you toss old floppies, reformat them, and stick 'em in your case. You won't regret it.

Carry Emergency Backups!

I know, I know: nothing's ever going to happen to *your* portable PC. You're not going to drop it, you're not going to lose it, no one's going to steal it, and it'll work forever. Sure.

But just to be on the safe side—consider this humoring me, if you prefer—why not carry a few floppy disks, no more than a half-dozen, as emergency back-ups to keep you computing, just in case . . . .

The most basic of those disks is a boot floppy. You need one of these at your desk, too, for your deskbound PC; but, as with almost everything else concerning portable PCs and the traveller, you *really* need it when you're away from the office. At your desk, you can call on a corps of potential helpers—a secretary or assistant, people in your company's Info Center or PC Support department, vendors' telephone help desks. On the road, too often *you* are your only resource.

A boot floppy is just what it sounds like: a bootable floppy disk, formatted with the DOS /S "System" command that moves the hidden startup files of DOS to the floppy. You should also copy the AUTOEXEC.BAT and CONFIG.SYS commands from your portable's hard disk to this boot floppy, and also any .EXE, .COM, and .SYS files that are called by those two files. Make sure COMMAND.COM is there, too. (Recent versions of MS-DOS automatically copy COMMAND.COM along with the invisible DOS files when you issue the FORMAT /S command; early versions did not. Make *certain* you have COMMAND.COM on your boot floppy, or you're not going to get far.)

If you have room left over—and with 1.44 MB floppies, you certainly should—add a few of the important external commands of DOS, such as

FORMAT and, if you use it, FASTOPEN. If you have still more space available on the boot floppy, find one or more of your most critical application programs that will fit on the disk, too, and copy it or them to the disk.

For the balance of your travelling emergency-backup set, copy those few remaining application programs (and associated files, such as print drivers) that you keep on your notebook or laptop PC, and which you really couldn't do without for a few days if your machine went down.

Again: you don't want more than a few disks. And make sure your copies are in standard DOS file format, not compressed copies created by a back-up program: you want to be able to stick these disks in a floppy-disk drive, run the programs and access the data directly from the floppies, if need be.

Now put a couple of rubber bands around those disks, stick them in a corner or pouch of your computer case, and forget about them. In the unlikely event that you do have a disastrous problem while you're travelling with that machine, you'll have a set of disks that can be used to

- boot up and work from, in the event the hard disk on your notebook or laptop goes awry;
- recreate the most important parts of your standard working environment and tools on a replacement or loaner laptop or notebook; and
- work at a borrowed desktop PC.

There: it's done. I hope you'll never need those disks. I'm *sure* you'll need those disks. And I'm certain you'll be glad you have them.

The Magic Box

Almost every serious portable-PC user I know travels with a small toolkit. Actually, that's a poor name, because it makes it sound like a set of hammers and saws. In practice, this little kit is just a handful of essential tools and gadgets—the gizmos you need when you have to work some magic on your PC. Many of the pieces in the kit are for making telecommunications hook-ups with the portable PC's modem easier, but some—such as a lightweight AC extension cord—are simply convenience tools, designed to ensure that the computer can be used in reasonable comfort in almost any setting.

Here's what you'll find in my portable-PC toolkit—my little Magic Box— these days:

Flashlight I always carry a tiny MiniMaglite, the smallest flashlight I've found that's really reliable, in my PC kit. You don't need much light—please, leave that Radio Shack five-D-cell hand torch at home!—but often you do need just a little light in the right place: on a telephone connection box mounted low on a wall behind a hotel bed, for example.

Just as important as reliability and general ruggedness is the security of the on-off switch. Before I found Maglites a few years ago, I was always taking out my old physician's-style penlight only to find it had gotten turned on by a bump in my computer bag . . . and the batteries were dead, their energy wasted illuminating some dusty corner of my bag for hours.

Maglites turn on and off by rotating the head of the light; it's almost impossible to turn one on by accident. There are Maglite-knockoffs available, too, some of which may be almost as good as the original, and plenty good enough for your Magic Box.

Leatherman tool Just as Maglites are the best of breed in flashlights, Leatherman tools are the *ne plus ultra* of multifunction pocket-sized tools. The original Leatherman, about the size of a common jackknife, is a stainless steel wonder that combines an extremely strong pair of long-nose, wirecutting pliers, a pocketknife, several sizes of screwdrivers (with both flat and Phillips heads), and an awl.

Unlike so many Swiss-Army-knife-style multifunction tools, the Leatherman's offerings are really stout, useful devices, which haven't sacrificed function and strength for collapsibility and pocketability. The Leatherman is fairly widely available; if you can't find one locally, call the mail-order outfitter, L. L. Bean, in Freeport, Maine.

Incidentally, there's a smaller, lighter, junior-sized Leatherman; stick with the full-sized model. The tools in the smaller model are acceptable, if not quite up to the standard set by the original model, but it's often hard to get a good grip on its smaller parts.

AC extension cord It's amazing how often you can't find an electrical outlet near where you want to work with your laptop or notebook. Or you'll find that the only available outlet is already full of plugs from floor lamps, table lamps, clock radios, and other devices. In hotel rooms, I marvel at how effectively designers manage to hide outlets behind beds and curtains, and at how carefully they calculate just the right the number of outlets to install in each room, to make certain none are left over for guests' use.

In offices and hotels, you can call the building manager's office or the concierge to get an extension cord sent up. I prefer not to wait the three hours it can take for them to show up with the cord, and so I carry a lightweight 25-foot AC extension cord with me. I emphasize *lightweight* here: it's hard to find light, two-pin cords in that length, but too often, shorter ones aren't long enough—and the heavy, three-pin grounded cords are out of the question.

Three-pin AC ground-adapter plugs Don't pull the third grounding pin out of the end of your PC's power cord. You're inviting electrical problems. Instead, carry a few of these cheater plugs. And remember that if you don't bother to connect the little wire hanging from the adapter to the center screw on the faceplate of the outlet to which you're connecting, you're throwing away a floating ground, just as if you'd ripped the grounding pin out of your power cord. (Do I really do this myself? Don't ask.)

Electricians' tape You'll find lots of uses for it on the road, in addition to dealing with telephone and electrical connections for your laptop or notebook PC—but let bailing you out of wiring problems be the excuse to pack a small role of plastic electrical tape in your Magic Box. (My favorite unauthorized use, so far: sticking the back part of my necktie to the front, when the little label on the tie that serves to keep the two pieces together, once tied, falls off unexpectedly.)

If you're an especially honorable person, you can also use the tape to repair any little tricks you've pulled, such as scraping insulation off the wires on a hotel telephone's hard-wired cord.

Telephone extension cord I actually carry *two* phone extension cords, in 25-foot and 6-foot lengths. The longer one is used to make the run to the invariably-inaccessible wall jack; the short one runs from my PC back to the house phone, so I can keep it connected.

Four double-female inline phone connectors These little double-ended connectors are worth their weight in gold. They allow you to connect two male phone plugs, a situation you'll run into more often than you'd expect. You might, for example, need to join your 25-foot and 6-foot phone cords to make an extremely long run. The connectors are available at every Radio Shack for a couple of bucks; carry several, so when you inevitably leave one behind, you've got a spare.

Two short telephone cords with alligator clips I use these to connect my portable PC's modem to telephones, telephone lines, and telephone boxes when I have to bypass a standard RJ-11 connector. You need only one, but the easiest way to make up one is to buy a standard 6-foot phone extension cord and cut it in half, then solder miniature alligator clips onto the red and green wires at each cut end; you'll get two short cords for your effort.

Those clips will then let you connect to any exposed piece of telephone wiring—in a telephone with its bottom cover-plate removed, to the permanently connected phone cord itself by scraping away a little of that cord's outside insulation, or to a telephone wall-jack with its cover plate removed. (You only need to make connections to the red and green wires; you can ignore the black and yellow ones and any others you may find in the cable.)

The other end of this short cheater cord plugs into the modem in my PC, and I'm in business.

This wouldn't be necessary if telephones weren't so often hard-wired into place, rather than being connected at one or the other ends of that cord by plugs and jacks. Unfortunately, too many people steal phones connected through jacks; you and I pay for their mischief.

Duplex connecting plug (Also called a "Y" connector, because it has two phone jacks on one side and a phone plug on the other.) This will allow you to connect both your portable PC and another telephone device—say, a portable fax machine—to the same phone line.

CP+ Connection (Also sold as a Konnex adapter.) Newer, all-digital telephone switchboards in many public buildings and hotels can defeat your best efforts to use your PC's modem. This little cheater box (see "Conquering Digital Phone Systems," in *The Complete Hotel Phone Hookup Guide*) lets you get through almost all of those systems.

Flat printer cable By carrying a printer cable—but not necessarily a portable printer—I can almost always borrow someone else's printer for a few minutes. People are wary of requests to unplug a cable from the back of their PCs so you can connect it for a few minutes to your machine; but they don't worry about you disconnecting the other end of that same cable from their printer for a while. (See "Do You Really Want To?" in *Printing on the Road* for lots more on this approach.)

DON'T TOUCH THIS! sign Over the years I've had some very unpleasant experiences with hotel maids who weren't sure what to make of my portable PC, jury-rigged to their house telephone system. One actually called a hotel's manager in a panic, thinking I must be sending some kind of spy reports off into the ether. Others have tidily unplugged everything, day after day, during my stay at the hotel—requiring me to dive back under the bed time and again to reconnect everything. And one pulled everything down into a heap on the floor, cracking the hinge on the display (but thankfully, not the display itself) on my laptop.

I try to avoid that now by carrying a couple of official-looking little 5 x 7-inch signs I made up in PageMaker and printed on garish yellow stock: they say *DON'T TOUCH THIS!*

Of course, when I use these signs I don't *know* that no one on the hotel's housekeeping staff touches the computer—but I haven't had any problems since I started using them. And since I retired from the KGB, of course.

The Complete Hotel Phone Hook-up Guide

Much of the power and usefulness of a travelling computer arise from its ability to be connected, via a telephone line, to other computers elsewhere. Yet plugging in and linking up on the road is far more difficult than it needs to be—or at least, it often SEEMS awfully difficult.

Here's a grab-bag of tips gathered from a few million miles travelling with a portable computer. Someday, none of this will be necessary as we come to rely on radio-wave connections when we travel. In the meantime, keep those wire-strippers and cheater cords handy; here's how to use them.

When It's Easy: Dataports

Sometimes, life is easy; then again, sometimes even the simplest things seem to conspire against us, and suddenly, life isn't so easy at all. For the PC-using traveller, one definition of "things going right" is when you find a "dataport" jack on the side of the telephone in your hotel room, or in an airline-club cubicle, or at another spot away from home where you're trying to use your notebook and its modem.

The notion of dataports is relatively new; we didn't see them before about 1989. By bringing the phone's connection to the building's telephone wiring out to an ordinary RJ-11 jack on the side or back of the phone, these instruments make it easy to hook up a PC. Instead of having to engage in guerilla action, you can simply set up your PC next to the phone, connect an ordinary phone cable from the modem jack on your PC to the dataport jack on the phone, and you're in business.

Usually.

Actually, while dataports look like they were planned as a convenience for the travelling computer-user, they emerged as a kind of defense against you and me. Hotel managers and others grew tired of finding we'd unplugged or disassembled their phones, or opened and left hanging the wires in a wall-jack, or scraped insulation off exposed phone wiring, or other acts of what they saw as vandalism against their precious phone systems. It was clear that more and more of us were going to be carrying and using portable PCs; it was clear that unless they did something, we'd soon have disassembled—and, they were sure, thus damaged—half the public-accommodation telephones in North America; it was clear they had to do . . . *something.*

The first dataport phones came from Comdial, the modern-day successor to the old Stromberg-Carlson radio company. A major producer of telephones, Comdial began offering major hotel chains phones with built-in PC-connection jacks. The first hotel in which I found a dataport phone was part of the Four Seasons chain (where dataport-equipped telephones are now standard), but I can't swear that they were the first to adopt this civilized compromise. Indeed, I've tried to track down the first hotel group to make the change—they deserve some kind of medal—without much success. History does not always reveal its most obscure secrets, even to intrepid reporters . . . .

At any rate, a dataport on a phone is always a good sign. Whether it works properly or not, and whether the hotel or other facility's switchboard works normally—or, like so many modern electronic switchboards, must be finessed by the PC user—it offers hope that you won't have to spend a half-hour crawling around under a bed or desk, trying to pry connections out of the wall and make your guerilla-computing hook-up.

When It's Not: On the Floor Again

So this time it's going to be messy: there isn't a dataport on the telephone. Here are some situations you're likely to run into, and how I tackle them:

With a Telephone Jack

It's almost as convenient to use your modem with a jack on the back of the telephone as with a dataport. You'll need to play a little game to have both your PC and the telephone available simultaneously—and you really don't want to give up quick access to the telephone, no matter how much you want to use your PC to send e-mail—but there's nothing difficult here.

Unplug the phone cord from its jack on the back of the telephone. Plug that cord into the LINE jack on your laptop or notebook PC's modem. Run a short telephone extension cord from the PHONE or OUT jack on your modem to that jack on the back of the telephone.

Alterativeły, you can unplug the phone cord from the phone, then connect the single-female end of a Y adapter to the plug on the end of the phone cord coming from the wall. Run a short telephone extension cord from one of the two phone jacks on the other end of the Y adapter to the

LINE jack on your modem, and run a second short extension cord from the other jack on the Y adapter to the telephone. (This strategy is sometimes necessary when the hotel's phone system uses on-site digital switching.)

Sometimes the phone cords used to plug into jacks in hotel phones have reduced-size tabs—the little tips you have to bend down with your fingernail to release the plugs. Of course, this is done precisely to make it more difficult for you to unplug the cord, in an effort to dissuade you from messing with the phone system. No problem: just use the tip of a knife blade or a small screwdriver blade's tip to reach in and depress the tab, then pull the cord and plug out.

If the phone cord doesn't plug into a jack on the back of your phone, but instead wriggles around underneath the phone, look carefully to see if it just makes a sharp turn in a recess in the baseplate of the phone, and then plugs into a standard telephone jack that's mounted within that baseplate recess. (This isn't done so much to keep you from meddling with the phone—though it sometimes has that effect on innocents—as it is to provide some strain relief by running the cord under a couple of tabs in the baseplate of the telephone, to keep it from being pulled out accidentally.)

If you run into that kind of setup, just unplug the cord from the jack—it may take a knife blade or screwdriver tip to reach in that far—and connect your PC in either of the ways described above.

All done—you can use the telephone in the usual way, and your PC's ready to start calling the world.

With a Wall Jack

This involves a little crawling around on the floor, but it's still easy.

If the phone wire comes straight out of the telephone without any sign of a jack and runs to a wall jack, just unplug the telephone cord from the wall jack, and plug the end of that cord into your modem's PHONE jack. Run a telephone extension cord from the wall-mounted phone jack to the LINE jack on your modem, and you're in business.

Just as with phone-mounted plugs, you may find a smaller release tab on these connectors; back to your trusty knife blade or screwdriver tip.

No Visible Jacks

Often, hotel phones are connected via a jack in the phone—but that jack is hidden from view under the phone's baseplate. Once again, management is trying to say it would be just as happy if you wouldn't fool around with their phones. *(Why are you staying in this dump . . . ?)*

If you suspect that may be so, just use the sturdy medium flat-tip screwdriver blade in your Leatherman tool or any other standard screwdriver to loosen the two, or at most three, screws that attach the baseplate to the phone. Don't detach any wires; just lift off the baseplate and set it aside. About 90 percent of the time, you'll find a nice, standard phone jack hiding under there.

Victory!

No Phone Jacks, Period

This is getting tedious. Now you must choose between electronic trickery or going to an acoustic coupler. I try to avoid acoustic connections, so I go after the phone's wiring.

Get out the little cheater cord you're carrying—the short cord with a phone plug on one end and two alligator clips soldered to the red and green wires which emerge from the other end. (You can safely ignore all other colored wires.)

If you don't mind losing easy use of the phone, unscrew the mouthpiece of the telephone handset and remove it, along with the microphone cartridge you'll probably find inside. You'll see a couple of thin wires running around inside that mouthpiece, one to the center connector for the microphone, one to the side. Clip the red wire in your cheater cord to the center tap, the green wire to the other. Make sure these jury-rigged connections are as secure as you can reasonably make them. Plug the other end of the cord into the LINE jack on your PC.

The phone won't be readily accessible for voice calls when you use this trick, so forget about plugging anything into the PHONE jack on the modem.

If you *do* mind losing access to the phone for voice calls, get out your pocketknife or Leatherman tool, open a small, sharp blade, and with the tip of the blade, very carefully run a straight, shallow slit lengthwise along about two inches of the phone cord, beginning about one inch from the point where the cord emerges from the base of the phone and running towards the wall. Don't cut too deeply: you just want to open this outer sleeve of insulating material, not cut into or even abrade the insulation on any of the wires inside.

When you've opened that slit, work your little finger or a ball pen under the four wires inside, and lift them out in a sort of inverted-U curve. Carefully scrape away about an eighth of an inch of insulation along both of the exposed red and green wires. Do *not* scrape insulation off both wires in the same place, but stagger your exposed wire sections, so they can't touch and short-out the phone circuit.

Now carefully slip the alligator clip on the red wire on your cheater cord onto the red wire in the phone cord; then connect the alligator clip on your cheater cord's green wire to the green wire in the phone cord. Plug the other end of your cheater into the LINE jack on your modem, and you're in business.

You can still use the telephone for normal calls. But be gentle when using the phone—and when using your PC, too, for that matter!—because it's all too easy to snap off those alligator clips, or even break the phone wires, when they're exposed and vulnerable.

If you use this trick, be a good guest and repair the phone cord before you check out. Wrap small pieces of electrical tape around each of those two bare places on the red and green wires; then wrap a longer piece of electrical cord along three or four inches of the phone cord itself, to seal the slit you cut and to provide some mechanical strength at what will be a weakened link in the connection. (And please: don't tell anyone where you learned to do all this.)

Acoustic Couplers

If you decide not to perform surgery, get out your acoustic coupler and hook it up. See "Acoustic Couplers," later in this section, for more information.

This little drill suggests an approach for the traveller who carries a PC and wants to use it and a modem on the road: find a chain of hotels with dataport-equipped room phones, and book there. Or at least, find one such hotel in each city you visit frequently and return to those hotels. At the very minimum, when you call to make a reservation, ask for the manager on duty ("M-O-D," in hotel parlance) and ask him or her if they have rooms equipped for computer modems. He may not know what you're talking about—a bad sign—but you may also get steered to a room where this kind of nonsense is not necessary.

And oh, yes: sleep well.

Conquering Digital Phone Systems

I can't say that it's always been easy to make a data connection through hotel phone systems—there's too much about the complications of these connections in this book for you to let me get away with that—but at least it hasn't been too bad, as long as you're willing to crawl around among the dust bunnies under the bed.

But now, digital telephone systems are adding a new and unpleasant wrinkle to the game.

The latest digital PBXs installed in hotels and other public buildings can make it very difficult to make a data connection. They're sensitive to signal levels and polarity in ways the older systems never were. And it's going to get worse: digital phone systems are clearly the wave of the future.

The best way I know to deal with these clunkers is via the little CP+ Connection, also known as the Konnex box. It's a tiny electronic cheater-box, designed solely to help defeat digital-telephone-system problems. The Connection/Konnex is sold by mail by CP+ and can also be found at some larger computer retailers.

You run a cord from the Connection to the handset cord's jack on the hotel telephone, then plug the handset cord into one end of the Connection. Another phone cord goes from the LINE jack on your PC's modem to the "data port" on the other end of the Connection.

One of the three switches on the Connection lets you choose between data and voice calls; in the latter position, the Connection is simply bypassed. A second switch affects data calls only; it can be set for *C* (standard one-line phone systems), *D* (electronic PBXs) or *E* (conventional, non-digital, multi-line phone systems). (But don't take those switch-position labels too literally; Northern Telecom's Meridian electronic PBX systems, for example, require that the data-call switch be in the *C*, or conventional position.)

There's also a polarity switch that can be used when the data-call switch is in the C position, to solve problems with the telephone wiring installed in the walls of the building. You'd be surprised how often, even in the newest structures, the polarity of the telephone wiring is reversed.

Feel free to fool around with switch settings: you can't hurt anything by experimenting with the switches on the Connection box, and eventually you'll probably be able to get out through most digital phone systems. This isn't foolproof; sometime there's just no way to get out. But at least the CP+ Connection/Konnex box gives you a fighting chance.

Isn't it perverse that in this digital age, using the most digital of tools, the personal computer, we're sometimes defeated by digital phone systems? Somebody oughta do something . . . .

Acoustic Couplers

Though today almost all modems sold for PCs are intended to be directly connected to a telephone system's wiring, acoustic couplers can still be handy tools. By eliminating the need for an electrical connection to the telephone's wiring, they often make it possible to make data calls through telephones otherwise unusable for modem calls.

Actually, acoustic couplers have a long history in the computer business. Back when most data communication over standard, dial-up telephone lines was at 50 bits per second (bps), and the really fast machines could link up at 300 bps, acoustic-coupled modems were the standard. Now, with 2,400 bps and 9,600 bps modems commonplace—and systems such as the Telebit QBlazer delivering an effective speed of 38,400 bps by combining fast transmissions with data compression—acoustic couplers have fallen by the wayside. Most acoustic couplers are unreliable beyond about 300 bps, and hardly anyone wants to put up with 300 bps today.

But Unlimited Systems' oddly named Konexx Koupler works at speeds up to and including 2,400 bps with most phone systems (including pay phones), and up to 9,600 bps with many electronic phone telephones. It's light and small, uses its own internal nine-volt battery (no "wall wart" AC power supply needed), and can be strapped to almost any telephone handset you're likely to find in a public place. The Koupler lists for $149, but you can usually find it for about $100 from computer discounters.

I don't think much of the Superman approach—diving into a phone booth, hooking up your laptop or notebook PC to the pay phone, dropping in your dime or quarter and firing off your latest missive to a waiting world. Indeed, most times when I see someone trying to use a portable PC with a pay phone I laugh, and wonder if they know how silly they look. But sometimes it really *is* necessary to make a data connection through a pay phone; at those moments, there's no alternative to an acoustic coupler like the Konexx device.

The Konexx isn't just for pay phones, of course. Given a choice, I'd always use a direct connection, rather than an acoustic coupling. But often travellers aren't given a choice; in those cases, the Koupler can save the day.

Leave It or Lock It Up?

I used to worry about the wisdom of leaving a portable computer sitting out in my hotel room when I'm travelling. It's not just that someone could steal it to sell for cash; it would be even easier for someone to slip into the room, read through the datafiles stored on the machine, maybe copy some to a floppy—or steal the computer for the value of the data on its hard disk, not just to fence to a local pawn shop.

I decided to stop worrying.

Most hotels will allow you to lock up your portable PC in their safe-deposit area—though not without some grumbling, because their safe deposit boxes are designed for smaller objects. But it's an incredible hassle to have to constantly unplug everything, haul the machine down-stairs, stash it . . . then retrieve it later, carry it back to your room, and reconnect everything again.

You could simply take the machine with you everywhere, of course—but that spoils a lot of social occasions, and increases the risk that it will be left in a taxi or knocked over by someone who never expected to find a computer at a cocktail party.

My solution has been to trust people and hope for the best on the theft issue. I stay in hotels that screen employees carefully and manage them closely, and that make it hard for outsiders to gain access to guest rooms. I've had a portable PC stolen from my hotel room once, so I know it does happen, and could happen to me again. But as portable PCs become more commonplace, and as their value falls, they're becoming less appealing to thieves, especially the kind of high-ticket felons who work hotels.

On the data-security front, I use a BSE portable hard disk (see "And Some Esoterica," in the "Buying Smart: Notebooks for the 90s" section of this book) for files which are even remotely sensitive and could cause problems if they strayed. The little BSE disk is easy to unplug from the computer's parallel port and stash in a conventional-size hotel safe deposit box when necessary.

Data security is an important issue for me as a consultant: client companies expect me to keep their information secure. Even when data seems innocent enough, its premature disclosure could cost my clients a bundle—and cost me my reputation. For me, a small, separate, self-powered, plug-it-in-anywhere hard disk is a good answer.

And for you, too, maybe.

Printing on the Road

All that bushwa about the "paperless office" has led some people to believe computers are bringing an end to the flood-tide of paper that washes across our desks. Not so; if anything, PCs have made it worse, by making it so much faster and easier to churn out a flurry of paperwork.

As much as we might like to escape from all that paper, the truth is that ink-on-paper communications are still the backbone of the business world. Which means that even the most future-minded PC-toting traveller still has to get it down on paper sometime. Here are the best ways.

Do You Really *Want* To?

The notion of having instant "hard," or paper, copy of anything you prepare on your PC is an appealing one. And an easy one to get used to. Especially when you have a printer at your elbow in the office, or available via your office's local-area network, the ease and presumed usefulness of simply hitting a key and seeing a nice, crisp printout of the work is habit-forming; before long, we come to see reducing our work to paper as the last, essential step in working at a PC.

Which means the travelling PC user, especially if he's new to the idea of using a notebook or laptop PC on the road, assumes he'll routinely need printouts of the work he does away from the office, just as he does at his desk. That's just not so, and falling victim to the *gotta have a printout* syndrome can lead you to waste a lot of energy—and a lot of money.

Good portable printers are widely available, at reasonable prices (see the next chapter)—and I use one from time to time—so I'm certainly not opposed to them. But I do find that most users of portable PCs—even the most active, avid notebook and laptop users—find they don't really need a portable printer, because they don't very often need printouts when they're away from the office.

So, while later in this section of the book I'll tell you which portable printers I think are best, give you some tips on choosing and using them, and also tell you about my all-time favorite sneaky trick for getting printouts away from they office *without* carrying a printer, let me first try to persuade you that you don't *want* a portable printer.

Much of the work most of us do on portable PCs doesn't require an immediate printout. We may, for example, be using that time otherwise lost when flying from point A to point B to get some work done—working on a draft of a proposal or report, or perhaps writing some quick memos to co-workers. We may keep our expense account for the current trip in a spreadsheet. We may use a database program to look up information we need to answer a client's question. Or we might use a complex financial model stored in the PC to come up with numbers clients and coworkers need—and maybe even then use the modelling program's graphics option to put together a quick graph or two of the results of those calculations, so it's immediately obvious what those numbers really *mean.*

But almost all of that work can be done, in its entirety, on the computer, without producing a paper copy . . . at least, until we get back to the office. You're not going to do anything with a printout of that draft report or proposal, for example, 'til you get home. You're not going to file your expense account 'til you get back. If you're just looking up data, you hardly need a printout of it right then. And even if you're working with a financial model in the company of clients or coworkers at a distant office, you may very well not need to—or *want* to—reduce your results to paper until you've had a chance to get back to the office and analyze the results more closely.

In the case of the memos to coworkers—and arguably, for every other item on that list—if you *do* need to get the information to others, you may very well do so by electronic mail, plugging your PC's modem into a phone line and sending the files immediately, rather than resorting to the old paper habit.

So you probably don't need to have a printer with you when you travel.

But, I confess, that isn't a complete answer, because yes, sometimes—not often, probably, but once in a while—you do need to get a printout quickly. But do you really want to carry a printer—a device perhaps as large and as heavy as your notebook PC itself—around with you all the time, just for those few times you really do need a printout?

There's a better answer: borrow someone else's printer. For years, I've carried a little parallel printer cable in the bottom of the case containing the portable PC of the moment. When I'm travelling and need the occasional quick printout, I just look around for someone in the office or hotel where I'm working who *does* have a PC printer. PCs are so ubiquitous these days that I never have to look far.

I ask that person if I can please use his or her printer for a moment. And I've never had someone refuse—thanks to that cable. Because if what I proposed to do was crawl around behind that person's PC, disconnect the printer cable from the PC, connect it to my little portable, print out my job, then crawl back behind the desk to reconnect the cable to the computer, I'd probably have drawn hundreds of "ummm . . . I don't think so."

In my experience, people think there's some kind of black magic in hooking things up to their computers. They finally got it working right—or *someone* finally got it right for them—and they don't want to risk not being able to get things reconnected properly.

Smart people.

Neither my experience and expertise nor yours are at issue here. It's not that the people whose assistance we seek think we're klutzes, it's just that they see that PC system as a mysterious and probably precarious thing, and who wants to take a chance that it won't work properly when this guy gets through with it?

After all, remember the time . . . ?

But when I say I just want to unplug the cable from their *printer* for a minute, plug my PC into it, and run off something, I never get any resistance. Because the magic, in peoples' minds, isn't in the printer, but in the PC. *Of course* they let me unplug something from that printer: it's a glorified typewriter! *What could go wrong?*

I don't want to deal with the roots of that view, nor argue with it, because I'm not much interested in psychoanalyzing people I ask for help. I just want to get my letter printed.

The printer cable I carry, incidentally, isn't one of those thick, heavy parallel printer cables found in computer stores. Those are much too bulky to carry around on a regular basis. Instead, I have a flat, six-foot "ribbon cable," made up with the proper connectors at each end for a PC and a parallel printer. Ribbon cables aren't designed for this kind of use, but for the much lighter duty of running from device to device inside your PC's chassis—from one add-in card, say, to another—and so they will eventually fail when hauled around like this. But they're cheap, incredibly compact and lightweight, and ideal for this kind of tuck-it-in-the-corner-of-your-bag-for-a-rainy-day use.

There's one more trick you need to know to make this work. You can never be sure just what kind of printer you'll be borrowing, so you want to make sure you have the right printer driver for your application programs (or for Windows, if you've succumbed to point-and-click computing). On the other hand, there are literally hundreds of different printer models, many of which require their own specific drivers. And you don't want to have to load hundreds of drivers on your portable PC's hard disk for each of the several programs you're likely to want to use on the road.

My answer is to load just six basic, widely interchangeable drivers for each program I use. I can almost always find among these one that will work properly with printers I borrow in the field. I keep drivers for the HP LaserJet II, Epson FX-85 and LQ, IBM ProPrinter II, and Okidata 93 printers, plus a generic Postscript printer driver, installed for each program I'm likely to need to print from. With those few choices, I can almost always get a decent-looking printout from a randomly chosen borrowed printer.

Windows, of course, promises to make all this a lot easier: by using just one printer driver to manage the output of all Windows applications, it eliminates the need to carry separate printer drivers for, say, such DOS programs as Lotus 1-2-3, Paradox, WordPerfect, Microsoft Word, HyperAccess 5, Magellan, Q&A, and so on. But unless you use Windows for *everything*, you'll need to carry proprietary drivers for DOS programs you still rely on.

If I haven't persuaded you that you don't really need printouts on the road, I hope you'll at least give some thought to this strategy of carrying a printer cable, not a printer, with you. You'll be amazed at how many kind people are perfectly happy to lend you their printer for a few minutes. *If* you promise not to mess with those wires coming out of the back of their PCs . . . .

Tiny Printers

If I haven't persuaded you that you don't want to carry a printer with you when you travel—and I don't want to by a hypocrite here, since I carry one myself sometimes—let's look at some of the choices available in truly portable PC printers.

Remember, as you consider these possibilities, that you could also buy and carry along a small desktop printer, such as the early HP inkjet units. I've included in my definition of "portable" here "battery-powered," but if you're sure you won't need to print when you're away from an AC outlet, there's no need to limit yourself to these few designs. Any one of a flock of very good and often very compact AC-only dot-matrix printers from Panasonic and Epson, for example, could serve well as portable printers if battery power isn't a requirement.

If you plan to print on the road only rarely, at sites where battery power isn't necessary, you could also rent a printer inexpensively at your destination when you know you'll be generating a lot of printed output. I've done this often, having a LaserJet II or similar unit delivered to my hotel suite for a couple of days. It's not expensive, I get no-compromises output, and I don't add an ounce to my travelling kit.

The first and most widely known and used portable printer came from Diconix, a division of Eastman Kodak. The Diconix has evolved through several models to today's extremely good Diconix 180si, which still has the small size and weight of its predecessors (about $6^1/_2 \times 11 \times 2$ inches, and 3½ pounds), as well as their inkjet technology. Over the years, Kodak has added a good-looking, built-in clone of the Helvetica typeface, as well as emulation of the IBM ProPrinter II and Epson FX85. The Diconix now also works well with Windows, and prints at about 25 characters per second.

Printed output is clean and crisp, thanks to the inkjet technology, but at 192 × 192 dots per inch (DPI), it falls well short of the "laser-printer look" many of us have gotten used to in printed output. That's about the resolution of a fax sent in fine resolution, so if you want an idea of how Diconix output will look, make a copy of one of your existing printed pages on your office fax machine, set at FINE.

The Diconix is neither the lightest nor the smallest of the portable printers, but it comes close on both fronts; it *is* the least expensive portable printer you'll find in general circulation, at $399 list (about $300 at typical street prices). It is also reasonably cheap to operate, which can be important if you plan to print very much while you're travelling. Operating costs are often a hidden *gotcha!* in portable PC printers, with per-page costs running to as much as $0.25 – $0.30 in some models. You'll get 250 pages out of the Diconix's $10 – $12 inkjet cartridge, for a much more reasonable cost of a nickel or so a page. As always with inkjet printers, the best results come from special paper, but the Diconix's output on decent-quality plain paper and letterhead stock is so good that I have trouble imagining anyone carrying special paper with them to feed into it.

The five built-in C-size nickel-cadmium batteries will give you about 25 pages per charge. (And these are standard, over-the-counter C-cell ni-cads, so you can replace them—or buy an extra set—locally, and cheaply. Many portable printers require expensive, nonstandard battery packs, available only from the printer vendor at ridiculously high prices.)

Overall, the Diconix remains my first choice for a small, light, battery-powered printer. But three other units are good alternatives; keep reading.

If printer size and weight are really critical for you, look at Citizen's PN48. A long, skinny box about the size of two boxes of business cards placed end to end, it offers extremely good 360 × 360 DPI printing using a thermal head and either single-use or multistrike thermal ribbons. At just a little over two pounds, it's the lightest printer I've ever seen. Built-in Courier and Times Roman fonts look good, even down through the very small type sizes the printer offers. The PN48 is fast, at 50-plus characters per second, and offers Epson LQ and IBM ProPrinter X24 emulations.

Citizen provides a proprietary nickel-cadmium battery pack which lasts for about 20 pages per charge. Expect to spend about \$0.20 – \$0.25 per page on the machine's pricey single-use thermal ribbons; you can save money by using the multistrike ribbons, but you won't like the results.

The Citizen lists for \$469; you'll pay about \$375 for it at street prices. That makes it a good choice for those who want the smallest and lightest possible unit, require very good quality output, and don't mind relatively high per-page printing costs. Make sure you carry extra ribbons; they're hard to find.

If you plan to print a *lot* on the road, consider Canon's Bubble Jet 10ex, the latest in this line of very good, fast portable printers. The Canon design is well thought out; overall, it forms more of a printing *system* than do the competition's offerings.

Output is 360 x 360 DPI, via ink jet cartridges. Unlike some others', the Canon ink jet cartridges will print on glossy stock such as overhead transparency material, without severe smearing problems (provided you give finished overheads time to dry before shuffling them together in a pile). That makes the Bubble Jet a good choice for boardroom warriors hitting the road. It weighs 4½ pounds and is about the size of a ream of letterhead paper.

Rated output speed at the high-quality setting is 83 characters per second. It's somewhat faster in draft mode, but stay with the high-quality setting; you won't like the results in draft mode. The Bubble Jet offers built-in Courier, Times, and Helvetica-like typefaces, and emulates the Epson LQ-510 and IBM ProPrinter X24e.

Built-in batteries last for about 25 – 30 pages. The inkjet cartridges deliver about 250 pages of text in high-quality mode, at about \$25 per hard-to-find cartridge, for a per-page cost of a dime or so. (Remember, though, that if you choose the Bubble Jet because of its very good graphics printing—again, perhaps for printing overhead transparencies—you'll get far fewer pages per ink cartridge than with straight text output.)

Most other portable printers are strictly hand-fed devices, accepting only single sheets of paper. The Bubble Jet offers a convenient, $90-list 30-page sheet-feeder option that works extremely well, though it adds noticeably to the printer's size.

The last of my favorite portable printers is relatively big, heavy, and expensive. But it's fast, produces beautiful results, and is a joy to use. Whether printing-on-the-go is worth its price in size, weight, and purchase price is up to you, but this is one of those PC peripherals that if you need it, *you need it.*

The machine is Mannesmann-Tally's MT-735. Think of it as a little LaserJet—and in fact, its biggest selling point is that it emulates the Hewlett-Packard LaserJet II, including 300 × 300 DPI output, LaserJet-quality full-page graphics, and compatibility with all the LaserJet downloadable typefaces. (A megabyte of RAM is one of its secrets, allowing those big images and downloadable fonts, as well as landscape printing of graphics.)

At six pages per minute—zippy for battery-powered printers—it even approaches the LaserJet II's output speed.

A built-in 80-sheet sheet feeder makes using the MT-735 for long documents a snap. And it includes ProPrinter X24 and Epson LQ-850 emulations, though for most users, of course, it's the LaserJet emulation that really counts. Thermal ribbons cost about $15 and produce 150 text pages; once again, carry extras, for you will not easily find these ribbons in computer or office supply stores.

Now for the bad news: The MT-735 is about $9^1/_2 \times 11^1/_2 \times 2^1/_2$ inches thick. Worse, it weighs a little over eight pounds. And it costs $1,295 list, about $1,000 on the street. Once again, whether it's worth the price in each of those ways depends a great deal on how you plan to use it. If you need what the MT-735 delivers, pony-up the grand and start building up the muscles in your right arm: there's nothing else like it.

Finally, I want to mention a printer I don't much like, but which can save the day for some PC users. All of the printers described so far are *non-impact devices:* that is, they melt or spray an image onto the page, almost noiselessly. That sounds wonderful—it *is* wonderful, when you're sitting in a hotel room at 2 A.M., silently printing out the final version of the proposal you and your team have been sweating over all day and must deliver in a few hours at a breakfast meeting— but has one severe limitation: non-impact printers cannot print multiple-part forms.

If part of your travelling routine involves printing snap-apart forms—say, purchase orders, or insurance proposals, or contracts, where you and the client must have identical copies—then you need an impact printer. And the only battery-powered impact printer I know that's worth using is Seikosha's innovative LT-20.

Unfortunately, most of what's innovative about the LT-20 is its form factor: it's a flat box, a little like an in-out letter tray, designed to sit beneath your notebook or laptop PC. It's also a relatively huge $14^1/_2 \times 11^1/_2$ inches, though only 2 inches thick; and it weighs a hefty 8 pounds. An automatic sheet feeder hides in that base, though sadly, it will only feed single sheets reliably, not the multi-part forms that are the machine's forte; you'll have to feed multi-part forms by hand.

Typefaces? A single, lonely, not-very-attractive Courier, which prints at 360 × 180 DPI, at about 50 characters per second. A $15-list ribbon cartridge lasts for 100 pages or so, producing an operating cost of about $0.15 per page. Built-in batteries last for about 35 – 40 pages. The LT-20 lists for $499, and can be found for just under $400.

If it were not for its ability to handle multi-part forms, the Seikosha wouldn't get serious consideration; it's a non-starter in most other ways, a generation behind the pack in battery-powered portable printers. But some PC users' needs include impact printing; if yours do, the LT-20 is your best choice.

Finally: Fax Yourself a Printout

OK: I tried to convince you not to carry a printer with you, but instead to borrow one locally as you need it. You wouldn't listen. Then I told you about four great portable printers (and one sorry but useful one). You didn't like any of them. So now I'm going to let you in on the greatest printing-on-the-road secret of all: faxing yourself hard copy of your documents.

If your notebook or laptop PC has a fax modem and fax software, it's easy to simply send yourself a fax when you need a printout—in a hotel, a client's office, an airline club, almost anywhere.

Depending on the quality of the fax software on your machine, the output may look even better than you'd get from any printer you're likely to be willing to carry with you. With one of the Windows-based fax-send software packages, such as Alien's FaxIt or Delrina's WinFax PRO, and Adobe Type Manager, you'll get a faxed printout that looks just like your onscreen version—and looks better than almost anything short of 300 × 300 dots-per-inch laser-printer output.

If you have only a simpler fax-send package running under DOS, it probably won't support typeset-look fonts and graphics, so the output may not be so spectacular. But it may very well still be acceptable.

Either way, you don't have to carry a thing with you, nor bother others to use their printers. In fact, because hotels rarely charge for incoming faxes, but only for outgoing ones, and colleagues and clients aren't going to charge you for receiving faxes on their machines, it probably won't cost you a dime to get that printout. Except the $2 tip for the bellman who brings the printout up to your room.

Even if you don't have a fax modem and software installed in your PC, you can still use this trick. Most of the third-party electronic mail services, such as MCI Mail, have a fax-send option. Just feed your file into the e-mail system through any standard modem, and the service will send your file to the fax machine you designate. You'll lose all special fonts and formatting, but that may not matter if all you need is a quick printout you can duplicate and share with others.

(If your fax arrives on that unfortunate, curly, murky, thermal paper still used by most fax machines, remember that you can slap those pages down on any plain-paper copier and get very good "plain-paper printouts" of the document—copies which usually look better than the thermal-paper originals.)

I use this trick constantly when I'm travelling. If you think of the five-million-plus fax machines in the world as nothing more than remote printers for your PC, you'll come up with even more ideas about how you can use faxing instead of printing to get—or distribute—hard copy of your PC-generated documents.

Slick, eh ?

Faxing on the Road

Fax machines would have become more important in our lives even without the impact of PC fax modems. But add the power of the computer to create, sort, store, and send fax messages—to one or a hundred recipients, at the touch of a key—and you have an irresistible combination.

Unfortunately, PC-fax systems still aren't very good replacements for stand-alone fax machines. The trick in using PC fax well is knowing when a PC-based answer is better than using a conventional fax machine. And the trick for portable-PC users is knowing how to navigate through the jungle of phone-line hook-ups, third-party fax forwarding services and other PC-fax options.

'Tis Better to Send Than to Receive

The advent of fax modems for PCs has brought about a small revolution in how faxes can be sent and received. The synergy between PCs and fax technology is obvious, and the convenience of being able to send and receive faxes from *portable* PCs is especially alluring. But unfortunately, not all the kinks have been worked out yet.

For a long time, fax machines (or in the older term, "telecopiers") were seen by office automation planners as a "bridge technology," something we'd get rid of as soon as we made the crossover to putting computers on most office workers' desks. The worldwide fax-machine population was holding steady in the neighborhood of one million machines, and the office-of-the-future gurus were eagerly waiting for fax technology to die.

But fax caught on like wildfire in the late 1980s, and confounded the pundits with its explosive growth. There are now about five million Group III-compatible fax machines (essentially, the only ones that count) in the world now, and that number is rising rapidly. Moreover, faxing caught on precisely because of what many had seen as its main limitation: its link to the world of paper documents. The notion of a "paperless office" is nonsense, at least for the foreseeable future; and so those whose forecasts of the passing of fax machines were tied to the demise of paper were doubly wrong. While many office workers are baffled by electronic mail, or simply don't have access to it, anyone can have access to an office's fax machine—and can learn to use it in about 30 seconds.

Put simply, fax isn't going away anytime soon.

The boom in PC fax modems grew out of a simple observation: in a lot of offices, many of the items which were being faxed originated in someone's PC. Given that, why then could we not skip the steps of printing a document, then feeding it through a fax machine's scanner, by simply digitizing the fax-format graphical image directly in the PC, then shipping the image out via a fax modem connected to that PC?

The GammaFAX, the first PC fax card, performed his task reasonably well, and an industry was born.

Unfortunately, while fax-sending hardware almost always works well, the software we use to manage that hardware has grown up along a painful and erratic path. Ideally, sending a fax from a PC should be just like printing the same document to paper: instead of choosing a printer as the destination, the user chooses a fax modem. The software handles the format conversion, then manages the transmission process, first with the PC's fax modem, and then with the fax machine to which the message is being sent. And this should all happen in the background, or at least from a fax spooler (analogous to a print spooler), so the PC user can go on with other work.

That's not a bad description of how PC faxing works on Apple Macintosh computers. With state-of-the-Mac-art fax modems, such as Global Village's TelePort units and the DoveFax, Mac users simply access the machine's Chooser, part of the Mac operating system, and designate the fax modem as the output device of choice. "Hot keys" make this even faster, through keyboard shortcuts.

Unfortunately, users of IBM PCs and compatibles have had a much tougher row to hoe. Available fax-sending software has lagged way behind PC fax hardware. Though many programs have offered pop-up fax access, few have done a very good job—which means a *largely transparent* job—of handling fax transmissions.

But times have changed, and the software we use today for sending faxes is a lot better. If you stay within the world of DOS, the software tools remain relatively crude. It's not impossible to get good-looking output on a distant fax machine, with just a reasonable amount of effort at your end—but you'll have to work at setting things up, and the process will be neither quick nor transparent.

Users of Windows are in a much better position, because all the best fax-sending packages—Delrina's WinFax PRO, for example—are Windows packages. That shouldn't be surprising: since faxes are themselves a graphical medium, a program that runs under a graphical system on the PC has an innate advantage. Moreover, Windows' method of allowing users to choose output devices, while slower and clumsier than the Mac's, can make the process easier. Finally, using Windows 3.1's built-in TrueType fonts and their associated rasterizer—or better still, using Adobe Type Manager and Postscript Type One fonts—makes it possible to send faxes from a PC which arrive at the addressee's fax machine with precisely the same type faces, type sizes, and formatting of the original document.

Intel, which has led the way in PC faxing through coprocessor-equipped PC fax modems (not yet available, sadly, for portables), calls this WYPIWYF, or "whippy-whiff": What You Print is What You Fax. In other words, if you can set up a document on your PC to print out a certain way, you can be sure it will appear on a distant fax machine in just the same way.

Which leads to a particularly useful view of fax machines: that they're really just remote printers for your PC—machines you can access just as you would a printer on your office network which happens to be on another floor, or in another department.

The only serious limitation here is output resolution. If you're used to seeing your letters and reports come off a laser printer in 300 × 300 dots-per-inch resolution, the 200 × 200 DPI of most fax cards (the fax standard's so-called "fine" resolution) will look a little shaggy. Still, the advantage of being able to print remotely to *anyone's* printer—that is, their fax machine—is an enormous advantage in business, and the relatively small loss in resolution is almost always insignificant.

Besides, faxes sent from your portable PC, at 200 × 200 DPI, will look so much better than the faxes your addressees receive from others, scanned through the lower resolution settings of most fax machines, that your work will still stand out.

The one remaining missing link in faxing from a PC is that the process only accommodates documents that originate in your PC. If you need to send something that's already on paper—a filled-in form, for example, or a signed contract, or perhaps a page clipped from a magazine—you're out of luck. (Strictly speaking this isn't so, because PC fax modems can accept input from external scanners. But the likelihood of carrying a scanner around with you is extremely small, and even in the office, few PC users use connected scanners to prepare documents for PC faxing: it's just too easy to use a conventional fax machine instead.) If you need to send faxes of paper documents when you're travelling, you'll still have to rely on borrowing (or renting, as with hotels' per-page fees for sending faxes for you) a fax machine along the way. Or you'll have to carry your own portable fax machine, which can be a very good idea. See "Portable Fax Machines," the next chapter in this section of the book.

You may have noticed that I've been talking here only about *sending* faxes, not receiving them, on PCs. That wasn't unintentional. The sad truth is that as convenient as portable PCs' fax modems can be for sending faxes, receiving faxes on any kind of PCs is a pain in the neck, almost always less successful than receiving them on standard fax machines.

The problem is that incoming faxes come in as huge graphics files. They take up big chunks of your hard disk. They have to be read onscreen with glorified (and sometimes, not even glorified) PC paint programs. They're hard to read onscreen, at best. If the fax was sent from a standard fax machine and was fed into that machine just a little skewed, the slightly-crooked image can be almost impossible to read on your machine's screen. And if the original was fed into the sending machine upside down—a common occurrence—you'll have to use a graphics utility to invert each page's image to read it.

Finally, faxes received on PCs lack one of the fundamental advantages of faxes received in the usual way: they aren't printouts, on paper, which you can mark up, fax to someone else with your comments, or file away.

So PC fax systems of whatever size and degree of portability are not very good all-round replacements for true fax machines. I use a fax modem frequently for sending material; but I try never to get in a situation where I have to receive faxes through my PC.

There is one special situation where receiving faxes via a portable PC can be an advantage. We're just starting to see a new generation of fax software which can run incoming faxes through a software-based digital OCR (optical character recognition) system, converting that big, dumb graphics image to standard ASCII text. Depending on how well the system works—and the early products, from Calera and Intel, work pretty well—this can be useful for filing away information received via fax in character form, where it can later be indexed, searched, and retrieved by such programs as Magellan and GoFER. And of course it can be very useful if you need to incorporate text received as a fax into a report of other document of your own creation; you just read in the text file and format it to look like part of your document.

But that's a niche market, and hardly lets PC fax off the hook for its maddening limitations as a receiving medium. I heartily recommend putting a fax modem—actually, a combination data-and-fax modem—into your laptop or notebook PC. But don't think that's going to free you from the tyranny of fax machines and wrinkly thermal-paper fax printouts.

You can receive faxes on your PC, but you won't like the results.

Portable Fax Machines

A lot of laptop and notebook PC users never think about this possibility, but a portable fax machine may prove a useful tool for those who send and receive a lot of faxes while travelling. I say this with some reluctance, because although the convenience of using a notebook PC for fax messages ought to be overwhelming, PC-faxing is still a long way from perfect. Receiving faxes is a mess, and eats up hard-disk storage; the process can be slow; and, for many PC users, it's still a confusing routine to send and receive faxes from portable PCs.

That's going to change—it *has* to change. But for now, if you really do send and receive a lot of faxes when you travel, and especially if you often find yourself faxing things that don't originate on your PC, such as newspaper clippings, annotated copies of other people's paperwork, pre-printed forms you've filled out, etc., a real fax machine is a lot more convenient and a lot more reliable than a PC with a fax modem.

Truly portable fax machines are hard to find. I exclude battery-powered fax machines from my definition of portable, because it's rare, indeed, that we need to send or receive faxes when we have no access to a standard telephone land-line and an AC outlet. If you do need that kind of capability, take a look at Mitsubishi's Acces battery-powered fax. It's not a great system, and you'll still have to track down a battery-powered cellular modem that works with fax protocols, but at least it's a start.

The best portable fax machine I've found is the Panasonic KX-F80. It fits into your attaché case, maybe even with room for a small notebook PC, too. In addition to the usual fax features, the F80 also functions as a standard telephone, has a built-in speakerphone, and also a built-in answering machine. Those are incredibly convenient features when you're stuck in a makeshift hotel-room office for a few days. It also has a "fine" setting for resolution, one-touch dialing, and auto redialing. Despite its tiny size and modest price—typically, under $500 at office-machine discounters—it's a tough traveller, and stands up to the rigors of bouncing along in your case.

I've often set up my F80 unattended in a hotel room, then let it auto-answer my calls, alternatively receiving faxes, passing them through to me, or recording messages. You may need to warn the hotel operator, and maybe your fax correspondents, too, about what you're doing, so an especially helpful operator doesn't vainly try to put through a call personally, yelling "Hello? *HELLO?!?*" into the fax machine's log-on wail.

Clearly, carrying a stand-alone fax machine as well as a notebook or laptop PC is overkill unless you really do send and receive a lot of faxes when you travel. But if you do, it's a lot better answer than struggling with the limitations of PC fax modems and software—and winding up searching for a standard fax machine, after all, when you have a paper document to send.

E-Mail Faxing Tricks

You don't really need a fax modem to send faxes from your PC. If you have an account with one of the popular third-party electronic mail services, such as MCI Mail or AT&T Mail, you can specify that outgoing messages be sent to any fax machine, properly formatted for printout there.

This is so easy that I often use it instead of a built-in fax modem or a fax machine. You're limited to plain text—and of course the material has to originate in your PC, as text, and not as a piece of paper—but it's so quick and easy that it soon becomes addictive. Note, too, that if you use e-mail a lot, and need to communicate with some people via e-mail who don't have e-mail accounts, or only have e-mail service through other providers to whom your service cannot easily pass messages, it's easy to specify fax delivery for those people.

Sending faxes via your e-mail service is also remarkably cheap. I use MCI Mail "Fax Dispatch" service, which charges by the half-page: for messages sent within the continental U.S., it's just $0.50 for the first half-page, and $0.30 for each additional half-page. Faxes to Alaska and Hawaii cost $0.80 for the first half-page, $0.30 for additional half-pages. Faxes to Canada are charged at $0.90 for the first half-page, $0.65 for each succeeding half-page.

There is no additional charge for the full-page cover sheets generated automatically by MCI Mail, for repeated retries if the receiving fax machine is busy or out of order, or for the receipts (or notices of cancellation, if the fax proves undeliverable) which are sent to your MCI Mail e-mail box. Compare those prices to your costs for printing out a message and sending it through your conventional fax machine, and you'll find they're very favorable.

You can also maintain fax distribution lists on MCI Mail without charge, and a single command lets you send identical faxes to everyone on one of these lists.

Faxing through e-mail services is often much cheaper than sending conventional faxes when your addressee is abroad. Examples of MCI Mail's pricing for the first half-page and succeeding half-pages, from the U.S.: to England, $1.50/$0.45; to Saudi Arabia, $3.65/$1.15; to Italy, $2.30/$1.00; to Argentina, $3.00/$1.00. The automatic retry and confirmation of receipt features are especially valuable in sending faxes abroad, as experienced fax users know: in many areas of the world, marginal telephone service makes faxing a hit-or-miss proposition.

Unfortunately, no e-mail service I know allows you *receive* faxes via your e-mail account. Such a system would be wonderful—especially when you're travelling—but it would have to be awfully sophisticated, doing on-the-fly conversion of incoming messages from the graphical fax format to e-mail's character format. It would also need to be able to detect and deal with real graphical images in incoming faxes—the photos, cartoons, rules around forms, and other material people send via fax machines—and that would be difficult to manage.

But there's hope. Executives at third-party e-mail services tell me they want to provide one-stop electronic communications systems for their subscribers, and they're working on the problem of receiving and translating incoming faxes.

Someday, someday . . . .

Power-Saving Tips

No matter how long a portable-PC manufacturer says the battery in your new notebook or laptop will last between charges, you know down deep that YOU never get that much service from it. You're right: vendors constantly over-spec battery life.

But even if battery capacities were magically doubled overnight, you'd still worry about running out of power, wouldn't you? You can do a lot to wring more life out of your present battery. Sensible battery-conservation techniques—whether built into your PC as user-selectable options, or simple, power-saving practices you can adopt—can make a huge difference in how long you work before your PC goes dark and silent. Here are the tricks you need to know to keep your machine running when you're at 30,000 feet and still two hours from LAX.

Screen Brightness

The single most effective thing you can do to extend the operating life of the battery in your portable PC is to turn down the display's backlighting. Or turn it off, if that's possible.

The various cold cathode systems used to edge-light portable PC displays suck up more power than any other component in the system's design. In fact, a display with its brightness turned up all the way probably draws more power than *everything* else running in the PC at that moment.

I used to keep laptop and notebook PC screens set on full brightness all the time. Then, as I began to think about the battery-life that can be gained by reducing the illumination level, I found I could work very happily at substantially lower levels. I can almost always see the display on the notebook and laptop PCs I use perfectly well with the backlighting turned down about halfway. In some cases I can turn it down even further.

This experiment hasn't just extended battery life-cycles for me; it's also made me more sensitive to the importance of contrast in LCD displays. I was often using very bright edge-lighting to compensate for low-contrast displays. Now I'm a lot pickier when choosing a laptop or notebook; I want high contrast and good visibility at much less than full brightness levels.

How much can you realistically expect to extend battery life by turning down the brightness? In a series of carefully controlled tests, I found I could extend battery life on three 386SX notebook computers by 20 to

30 percent by reducing screen brightness by about half. In practical terms, that means I was turning $2^1/_2$-hour batteries into 3-hour-plus batteries—a real improvement.

New PCs using the 386SL chip from Intel will offer even more dramatic improvements, as manufacturers learn how to access the power-saving tricks built into the chip. For now, dimming the screen down to a workable—if less than dazzling—level will pay big rewards in terms of working longer between charges.

Built-in Power-Saving Tools

Turning down screen brightness is a brute force method of extending battery life in your portable PC. Using the sophisticated power-management tools built into many current notebook PCs is a much more elegant solution to the problem. These machines typically use a pop-up screen to allow you to set up your personal power-saving preferences. You can change the values at any time.

After screen brightness settings, the biggest contribution you can make to extending battery life is to allow the PC to shut down access to its hard disk every now and then. Normally, hard disks spin continually; that makes for fast data access. If the disk isn't constantly spinning, it has to come up to its specified rotational speed before the magnetic heads can move across its surface to read the data your application program is seeking. Built-in power-conservation programs allow you to set the interval before the hard disk stops spinning. The shorter the period before the disk stops, the greater the power conservation.

That's the disk-power conundrum: you can save power by turning off the disk when it's not being used frequently . . . but at the price of slower disk performance.

In practice, you may not notice much difference in performance if the program you're using doesn't access the disk very often. And of course programs that keep their code plus your data in memory at all times (such as the word processor Eye Relief, discussed elsewhere in the book) won't slow down at all. On the other hand, programs such as database managers, which are constantly reading from the disk during look-ups, will perform much more slowly when a short interval before hard-disk shutdown is specified.

You won't need to turn the disk back on again; the first time your program tries to read from or write to the disk, power is automatically restored to it.

Power-management programs also typically allow you to set a time-out interval for the display. While you can work with many programs while the disk is shut off, you certainly won't want to work on a PC whose a display is constantly flickering between bright and dim; this setting is intended to reduce screen brightness when you walk away from the computer for a few minutes, or look off into the distance to think Deep Thoughts. Screen time-out periods are typically much longer than disk time-out cycles, and thus contribute somewhat less to overall power conservation.

The latest notebook PCs, using Intel's 386SL chip, can shift gears on microprocessor speed, slowing down the chip itself when you're not actually using it—or keeping it running constantly but at a slower speed, for those applications, such as word processing, where CPU performance isn't so important.

Turning off current to a built-in modem is another important power-saving trick offered by many power-management programs. Most portables' modems place a constant low-level draw on the system's batteries; switching the modem off, manually or automatically, makes a small but useful difference if you use your PC a lot, a very large difference if it's sometimes a week or so between uses.

Finally, well-designed built-in power-conservation systems override these settings when they detect that AC power is being supplied to your computer.

If your notebook PC doesn't have these features, there's no way to add them. If your present machine does include any or all of these, use them prudently and you'll extend battery life by 10 to perhaps 40 percent without a serious penalty in performance.

And if you're shopping for a new machine, look closely at the nature and extent of its power management features. "Smart" PC power-conservation systems can make a big difference in battery life.

Remote Computing

No matter how carefully you download files from your desktop PC to your notebook for the trip to Memphis, you always worry that you won't remember everything you may need. Worse, no matter how carefully you choose the files to download, you know that once you get to Memphis, you're going to realize you should have brought the XXXX.DOC file, as well. Or a question from the Memphis client will make you realize that if only you'd brought the ZZZZ.WK2 file, you could close the deal right then.

Remote computing makes it possible to retrieve files from your desktop machine from afar, and also to run programs resident on your desktop machine remotely. It's a nice trick, and it's surprisingly easy.

Remote Access: Perils and Rewards

One of the slickest things in the experienced portable PC user's bag of tricks is the capability to call a distant PC from a laptop or notebook and connect the two. Then it's possible to transfer files from one machine to the other—sending reports written in the field back to the office, for example, with elaborate formatting fully intact, to be printed and distributed. Or even loading and running a program on the distant PC and watching it work on your portable's screen.

Consider the usefulness of being able to call your desktop PC from your notebook, for example, run a CD-ROM search program, and look up some data on a CD-ROM disk you left in that deskbound drive when you departed.

That's hot stuff for today's portable PC user, and it's easy and inexpensive to set up, easy to use.

As I suggested in the previous chapter, you should decide first whether you're going to make Windows-to-Windows connections, or DOS-to-DOS connections. I'll discuss good software for both scenarios, but let's focus on DOS-to-DOS sessions for now.

And before we begin, you should decide what you really want from remote access. If all you'll need is the ability to download to your portable a file or two or ten that are resident on your desktop machine—or to reverse the process, sending back to your office PC some work you've done on the road on your portable—then read no further. What you want isn't remote-control software, but a file-transfer program capable of running over modems and dial-up phone lines. The classic example of that kind of program is LapLink Pro. See "File Transfer Utilities and More," in "Transferring Files," later in the book.

Remote-control software usually comes in "dual packs," with different versions of the program for the host (deskbound) and guest (portable) PCs. The host program controls the process—setting up access privileges, for example, such as passwords for those authorized to log on from afar. Never try to do an end-run around password protection; you don't want your desktop PC left vulnerable to a malicious hacker who just may try your number, wiggle into your system, then start reading—or erasing—your files.

Indeed, the best remote-control programs back up password-access systems with a dial-back option. When a desktop PC running the remote control program receives a call and digests the password offered by the calling machine, it then disconnects, looks for that password in a hidden table, and finds a call-back number associated with it. It then calls that number—where, presumably, the would-be remote user is sitting waiting, his PC running his copy of the remote-control package and his PC's modem in auto-answer mode. The guest PC answers the call-back, the two machines are linked, and the user goes to work.

Unfortunately, dial-back systems, as useful as they are conceptually, often don't work well in the real world of travelling PC users. The problem is that the typical laptop or notebook user is on the move, not always calling from that same, preregistered telephone number. And of course he can't change the remote number in his first call, because that would defeat the security aspects of the feature . . . .

Dial-back systems also don't work when you have to leave a switchboard number: what is a hotel's PBX operator supposed to do when she answers the hotel's main number and a distant computer starts whistling at her?

All of which means you want to set up a good password system—please, no easy-to-remember but dumb passwords like "a," or "WOW," or "today" or any of 20 or 30 other easy-to-guess choices—and rely on it for your security.

A second issue in setting up a successful remote-control access system is putting the right modems on both PCs. Remote-control systems have to ship a lot of data back and forth: not just the information you see onscreen, but the background "overhead" code necessary to manage the process. Good remote-control software makes aggressive use of data compression before sending files and after they're received, but it still wants to find a fast modem.

The usual 2,400 bps modem is marginal at best for remote use. You want at least a true 9,600 bps modem; and faster units, such as the new class of 14,400 bps V.32bis-standard modems, or screamers such as the Telebit QBlazer praised elsewhere in this book, are even better. You probably won't be able to get an internal modem for your notebook or laptop PC that meets those specs, so you'll have to carry an external unit.

Still, the convenience of remote access to and control over a desktop PC is so great that it's worth the hassle.

Which remote-control packages are best?

Norton Lambert's Close-Up is the best all-round remote software package I've used. It's fast; it's easy to install, set up and use; and it does smart things like checking to see if a file to be transferred has already been compressed, so it doesn't attempt the job twice. Expect to pay about $125 – $135 for a dual-pack of Close-Up.

If you want to work in Windows remotely, look at CO/Session, from Triton. Close-Up handles Windows acceptably, but CO/Session is optimized for the Windows environment. The great advantage held by CO/Session is what Triton calls "Intelligent Graphics." That's the name for Triton's proprietary technique of sending as little code as possible, instead of full-screen bitmaps, under Windows. CO/Session also has very sophisticated security functions.

CO/Session also costs about $135 per dual pack, at typical street prices.

Unlike CO/Session, which is a DOS application that works well with Windows, another choice, Carbon Copy for Windows, is a Windows application itself, which offers the appeal of a graphical interface. My biggest reservation about Carbon Copy for Windows is how it handles DOS programs. It cannot run them full-screen (as you can, easily, under Windows itself). Instead, it can run them only when Windows is running in its 386 Enhanced mode (not a problem), where it runs DOS programs only in a window (often, a very large problem, especially on the relatively small displays of notebook and laptop PCs, resulting in tiny, hard-to-read characters).

As useful as remote computing can be, I have to warn you about its limitations. Ideally, we'd like to be able to log onto our desktop computers through a modem and remote-control software, then use that distant desktop machine just as if it were sitting next to us. We could run any program, create files, and generally use the distant machine as if we were sitting in front of it.

That's the *promise* of remote computing.

The reality of remote computing, unfortunately, is that sending information back and forth over phone lines is so slow that you'll go crazy if, say, you call in, load your word processor, and try to write a report.

Running a program on the distant machine is perfectly possible, technically, and is often very useful in a practical sense, too. For example, I can call my office PC, run Paradox, and look up a client's name and account status in just a few seconds. That's because almost all of the actual processing takes place at my desktop machine, and very little actual information is shipped back and forth.

I can even write a change into record. But I'd never try using Paradox from afar for a long session of database work—say, extracting a series of records, formatting them into a report, and printing it. That would be agonizingly slow.

A related problem with controlling program execution on your desktop PC from afar is the slowness of managing non-Windows graphical screens. Using something like Harvard Graphics remotely, or Microsoft Word running in its graphics mode, is like chewing a mouthful of taffy: it takes forever.

If you have realistic expectations for remote access to your desktop computer, you'll be delighted with the results from any of these programs (including LapLink Pro for simple file transfers). But if you have in mind large-scale computing projects run from afar, don't set yourself up for a disappointment: it just won't work.

The Windows Issue Again

We have to circle back to the DOS versus Windows issue one more time. But only briefly.

If you want to access your desktop PC from your laptop or notebook when you're away from the office—and being able to do so can range from a wonderful convenience to an absolute lifesaver—you should decide first whether or not you need to call a desktop machine running Windows, or not. Your decision will shape the kind of remote-control software you buy, and will profoundly shape the performance of those modem-to-modem remote connections.

You guessed it: Windows links will run slower. A *lot* slower. I mean, *A LOT* slower . . . .

But if you need 'em, they're available.

By contrast, DOS-to-DOS link-ups are relatively quick and easy to manage. They're far more efficient and somewhat more stable.

Here's why. When you dial into a machine running Windows, and start manipulating things, the remote-control software has to pass those huge Windows screen images back and forth, so you can see what's going on the other computer. The best Windows remote control software (see the next chapter) does that relatively efficiently, not sending full-screen bitmaps back and forth every time, but only the code needed to redraw the changed parts of the screen.

But it's still a slower process than just sending new lines, as in DOS.

Windows remote-control programs are also hobbled to some extent by Windows' own sloppy management of a PC's serial ports. Though remote-control programs need every bit of speed they can get—and in addition to internal data-compression/decompression routines, try to drive modems at a minimum of 9,600 bps, and usually much faster—Windows is too dumb to handle serial port speeds faster than 9,600 bps without losing data. So the communications software is trapped by one of Windows' most egregious pieces of bad coding.

My answer is simple: I try, even on machines on which I usually run Windows, to handle remote work from within DOS. If the dream of remote computing held true—that I could dial in from anywhere, execute a program on my desktop computer, see on my portable's screen what was going on, then work in that desktop program just as quickly and comfortably as if I were sitting at my desk—then that would be a loss, because I like a lot of Windows programs, and I'd like to be able to use them remotely.

Unfortunately, as you'll soon see, remote-control software is fine for transferring files from one of the two connected PCs to the other, and OK for the occasional brief execution of a program on the distant computer, with the results reported to your portable's screen. But it's just not up to doing something like building a spreadsheet or writing a word-processing document on the remote machine. No matter how patient you are, I can guarantee that you're not *that* patient. And that's as true for DOS connections as for Windows sessions.

So if you can swing it, consider doing your remote computing in DOS. If you can't—if your desktop PC is always running Windows, for example, and you don't want to change that—then there are a couple of interesting Windows remote-control packages.

But you should understand the performance hit you're taking.

III.

AT YOUR DESK

The Desktop-Notebook Workstation

Whether you use, or intend to use, a notebook or laptop PC to extend the power of your desktop PC to the work you perform away from the office, or want to make that portable PC your ONLY computer, there are little-known products and little-known tricks that can make your life a lot easier.

For the two-PC user, moving files back and forth becomes routine. But how do you make sure you've always got the latest version of a file . . . on the right machine? For the notebook user who's made that machine his or her only computer, backing up files is more important than ever. But how do you handle back-ups from a notebook?

Here are some tips and tricks that will safeguard your data and your sanity, no matter which approach you choose.

Civilizing the Workstation

If you like the notion of using your laptop or notebook PC as your *only* PC—using it at your desk as well as when you're travelling—you'll want to reduce or eliminate any compromises in desktop computing power and convenience caused by your decision. In fact, the overwhelming advantages of having just one computer, with just one set of programs and data files, is such a convenience itself, you won't have much to worry about: you're already way ahead of the game. But it's easy enough to iron out the few wrinkles that exist in the notebook or laptop-PC desktop workstation.

One essential step is to duplicate a few tools on the desktop. If you use a mouse with your PC, leave your "travelling mouse" in your computer case where you're working with the computer at your desk; get a second, identical mouse for desktop use. Otherwise you'll spend too much time digging it out, then packing it away again—with the inevitable result that you'll wake up some morning in San Diego and remember that your mouse is sitting on your desk back in Toronto.

Similarly, buy a duplicate power supply/battery charger, and an extra AC power cord, both of which remain at your desk. Again, you don't want to have to pack and unpack any more than necessary, and you *really* don't want to wind up on the road with no way to charge your portable's batteries.

Though it's perfectly possible to work at your desk with a portable PC's built-in keyboard and display, I prefer to keep a separate conventional monitor and a standard keyboard on my desk. That way I have the benefits of a large, high-resolution screen, and the touch and convenience of a full-sized keyboard, when I'm in for a long period of work at the computer in the office.

This may seem a little wasteful to you—and perhaps to your boss or purchasing agent, as well. After all, if the keyboard and display in your portable are good enough to use on the road, why aren't they good enough to use in the office? The answer, of course, is that if you could have the advantages of a bright, sharp, full-sized color monitor, and a full-sized, full-keystroke-travel PC in your portable, without any size or weight penalty, you'd choose that in an instant.

But you can't; portable PCs are built around reasonable compromises. Try to do without a separate, standard keyboard and monitor at your desk and you'll probably begin to have second thoughts about this idea of using a portable PC as your only PC. Don't succumb to that; buy the monitor and keyboard.

You also want easy connection to your office printer, and to the office's local-area network. Leave a longer-than-usual parallel cable attached to your printer, with the PC end of the cable held securely in a little clamp atop your desk. I've used a pipe stand for this with great success; I've also seen rubber stamp racks used for this purpose. Fancier systems are available, but they don't work any better. Keep the pocket LAN adapter you use to hook your laptop or notebook into the network, and the AC power cord for the portable PC, in that little rack as well.

You don't want to have to crawl around on your knees under or behind your desk every time you return to the office and need to reconnect those three cables.

If you use an external modem with your portable PC and have a separate telephone line at your desk for a modem (rather than using a serial port to connect to a shared modem through a telephone system or the local-area network), consider buying an extra modem for use at your desk. At minimum, get an extra AC power supply for your travelling modem and leave it plugged into an AC outlet at your desk, its modem connector trapped in your pipe rack or other "holding pen" along with the printer, network, and computer power cords.

Never, *ever* dip into your Magic Box of road tools to work on something at the office. Buy duplicates of any of those tools you think you may need at your office, and keep them in a desk drawer. I can guarantee that if you swipe something from your travelling kit to use for just a minute at your desk, the next time you need that tool or gizmo when you're on the road, it'll be sitting in the office.

The point here is clear, I hope: Don't let using a notebook or laptop PC in the office become a hassle. And don't strip critical elements out of your travelling kit, only to forget them next time you grab your PC and run to the airport.

Finally, I strongly recommend that you set up a permanent back-up system at your desk. I discuss backing up portable PCs' hard disks elsewhere in this book; whichever back-up strategy you choose, make sure the tools to use that system are readily at hand on your desktop.

If you feel you need an additional hard disk, or a dedicated tape, optical-disk or cartridge backup system, or another major external component at your desk, consider getting a desktop docking station for your portable PC. I generally find docking stations clumsy and more trouble than they're worth—not to mention their exorbitant cost. But once you start having to plug too many things into your portable PC when you put it on your desk—and unplugging them all when you travel—the wisdom of using just one PC inside as well as outside the office may seem a little dubious.

Docking stations may offer a good answer for some PC users; see the next chapter.

Choosing a Docking Station

Docking stations are an effort to bridge the worlds of the portable computer and the desktop computer. By making the connection of external devices, such as a monitor and keyboard, easier, docking stations at least theoretically make life simpler for the one-PC owner.

The problem is that good docking stations are few and far between. Most are no more convenient than making those connections one at a time by hand. Most offer too few expansion slots, drive bays, and other PC-expansion possibilities to make a real difference. And most just get in the way on your desktop, eliminating the space savings you'd expect from using a compact notebook or laptop PC instead of a hulking desktop machine—and making the real desk-clearing trick of simply moving the computer elsewhere for a few minutes impossible.

Still, there are some arguments in favor of desktop docking stations. Making more than three or four connections when you bring your notebook to your desk, or when you liberate the computer for road duty, gets old. If you count connecting a monitor, keyboard, AC power supply, and printer as basic steps, plus a network adapter as a near-necessity, we're already past that point. Add such touches as an external modem's serial cable, a SCSI connection for a CD-ROM player, and maybe a tape back-up unit, and it can get pretty tedious.

So as much as I dislike the clumsiness of docking stations, they probably have their place.

Computer buyers apparently agree: Compaq says almost a third as many docking stations have been sold for its portable PCs in the SLT and LTE/LTE Lite series as the computers themselves. People are obviously plugging a lot of Compaqs into docking stations—or at least, buying docking stations because they think they'll use them. Toshiba, NEC, Texas Instruments, and other notebook and laptop PC makers who offer docking stations don't report nearly such high penetration; maybe this is a counting problem.

Or maybe Compaq has a better product.

In fact, I think Compaq's most recent docking stations, for its LTE Lite computers, are the best I've seen. In the compromise between the Battleship Docker approach, which tries to accommodate everything imaginable but nearly needs a desk to itself, and the minimalist designs, such as Texas Instruments' compact sidecar-style boxes, which take little space and provide little value, Compaq's design tilts towards the battleship side, but at least gives you back a lot of functionality for the real estate it commands.

Like most other products from Compaq, their docking station—oops, the Desktop Expansion Base—is well designed, in many ways *over*designed. But it gives the user a lot of flexibility. It offers push-in, one-connector convenience when you bring your Compaq notebook to the unit, and equally quick and easy disconnection. The expansion base has two ISA expansion slots, accepts one one-third-height and one one-half-height drive, and, unlike some docking stations, allows you to open the lid of the computer and use the built-in screen if you wish. It will even allow you to type on the notebook's own keyboard, as well . . . but you wouldn't want to, because it sits up several inches higher than your desk surface.

If you don't want to use the internal display in a Compaq LTE Lite, a sturdy, tray-like lid fits over the top of the expansion base, forming a solid platform for most medium-sized monitors. There's direct pass-through of all the portable PC's connectors to a desktop-PC-style back panel, and even a key-lock arrangement that lets you lock your portable into place.

If you do lock your portable into the expansion base, no one's going to steal the combination: it's big and heavy, actually larger than some Compaq desktop PCs. The base alone weighs 19 pounds, and is 16 inches wide, 14 inches front to back. Without an external monitor, it stands about 7 inches above your desk. Add a Compaq LTE Lite, and the combination pushes 25 pounds. *(Excuse me: are we still in the world of small, lightweight notebook computers here?)*

But the Compaq Desktop Expansion Base does work, and works well; if you have a Compaq LTE or LTE Lite, take a look. Bring your checkbook: it'll set you back $1,000 or so.

NEC—which claims to have invented the concept of docking stations, and once tried to claim the rights to the term —has an oddball docking station for its splendid Ultralite III monochrome and Ultralite 25slc color notebooks. With NEC's unit, you can latch the notebook into the docking station, then carry the *whole thing* along with a sturdy handle, like a small suitcase. You won't want to do that—it's a dopey idea—but it is an interesting engineering concept. You can, of course, also simply use the unit, NEC notebook PC in place, atop your desk.

Toshiba's most recent docking stations are interesting exercises in computer engineering, as well. Similar in concept to the Compaq base but smaller and simpler, they allow fast and easy insertion and removal of Toshiba's high-end notebooks. Overall, they are lighter and less clumsy than Compaq's system, but offer somewhat more limited flexibility.

If you're a confirmed minimalist, you'll probably love the brand-new Zenith Readydesk Port Replicator. Don't worry: the product is a lot better than the name. It's a simple, slender strip that fits across the back of Zenith's Z•note notebook PCs, and literally replicates all of the machine's ports for connecting external devices, bringing those ports out to a set of duplicate connectors on the back of the Readydesk.

The idea? You leave the Readydesk sitting at your desk, with all those external devices' cables plugged into it. When you bring your notebook to your desk, a quick, simple, one-step plug-in gets everything connected in just a second or two. And when you get ready to go, you have the convenience of similar, one-step-disconnect.

If you're as offended as I am by the idea of spending $1,000 on a conventional docking station, the much more sensible $150 list price of the Readydesk should sound pretty good, too.

If I seem less than impressed with the idea of using a docking station, it's simply because I find them so klutzy that they tend to defeat the grab-it-and-go idea behind using just one PC, whether you're at your desk or on the road. In the end, after examining and working with a wide range of docking stations, I prefer doing without one, and doing a little more plugging and unplugging myself, so that I can simply stand my notebook PC in a little rack on my desk. My rack was made for me at a plastics hobby shop from heat-formed Lucite, and does nothing more than hold the notebook upright, front-edge down, so I have easy access to its side- and back-mounted connectors.

I'm convinced that if portable PC makers offered such simple devices, at $25 – $50 per, lots of their users would go for them. Or if a third-party outfit developed a line of simple stands, sized to fit popular notebooks, they'd find a worthwhile market.

Most existing docking stations seem to me a thousand-dollar answer to a fifty-dollar problem. There's got to be a better way.

Transferring Files

The two-PC user quickly comes to accept the need to move files back and forth from one machine to another. Whether by cable, disk, e-mail, remote PC link or LAN, keeping the most-recent version of data files on the machine being used at the moment is critical.

But transferring files between computers isn't just an issue for the person moving constantly between a desktop PC and a portable machine. Even the portable-only PC user has at least an occasional need to exchange data files with colleagues and clients—sometimes in the office, at least as often for many, on the road, in someone else's office.

Transferring files is easy; choosing the right method often isn't. Here's what you need to know to make quick and easy transfers every time.

Floppy-Swapping

Once upon a time, in a cold and thankfully distant world which didn't yet have local-area networks, we called the practice of copying files onto floppy disks and carrying them down the hall to someone else who needed to use them "sneaker net." It was a regular part of the daily routine for many PC users, and all that floppy-shuffling got pretty old.

Today, many laptop and notebook PC users have adopted the same way of moving files between their portable and desktop computers. They may not move from their chairs as they do the floppy shuffle, but the principle is the same, and the process is just about as tedious.

I'll agree that it's unquestionably easier to use a floppy-disk transfer to move one or two files from portable computer A to desktop computer B, than it is to hook up a cable between the two machines and run copies of a file transfer program on both machines. Or to have to plug your portable PC into the network, log-on, then transfer files over the LAN. No matter how hard you try to make those processes convenient, they're still slower than a quick disk transfer.

But if you're transferring more than a couple of files, the floppy shuffle gets old fast, and the other approaches become a lot more appealing.

The one situation where larger-scale floppy transfers may make sense is when you're moving files between two computers at different locations—say, between a notebook PC you keep at home and travel with, but never carry to the office, and your desktop machine. Even there, I'd argue that if you make those transfers often, and many files are involved, shipping the files back and forth by modem may be easier.

For some PC users, the notion of setting up a file-transfer program and dealing with the necessary cable connections is a little intimidating. And a surprising number of PC users who work every day with programs and files across a local-area network tell me they're still confused about how to use the network, and never do much beyond running their own few programs and sending output to network printers.

Trust me: if you often need to move more than just a few files at a time and are still shuffling everything from one machine to the other via floppies, you're living in the past. Learn to use the file-transfer capabilities of your network or, better still, get a file-transfer program such as LapLink Pro and spend the five minutes it takes to install and learn to use it.

File-Transfer Utilities and More

Local-communications packages, such as Travelling Software's LapLink, make the lives of portable PC users a lot simpler. By enabling fast, easy file transfers between two dissimilar computers, they can eliminate the floppy shuffle. These programs also have other uses—for example, creating a *de facto* two-machine network, or setting up new notebook or laptop PCs to exactly match the software configuration of a company-standard portable machine, by copying software from that stock setup, complete with a directory structure, to the new machine. But they exist mainly to manage file transfers between portable and deskbound PCs, and they do that job superbly.

LapLink and Brooklyn Bridge were first in this field, but are hardly alone. Other packages, such as FastLynx, Direc-Link and HotWire, also gained followers. I continue to use LapLink—now in version four, called LapLink Professional—because it has everything I need, and I've come to trust it.

LapLink's best feature is its auto-installation "self-cloning" routine. Connect a PC—any PC, desktop, laptop, or notebook—that's running LapLink to any other PC. Tell LapLink to try to establish a connection between the two. If LapLink then detects that there is not a copy of the program installed on the second computer—making connection impossible—it asks if you'd like to copy LapLink onto that machine. If you say yes, LapLink sets up a connection using DOS's primitive file-transfer facilities, then installs itself on the new machine. When the installation is complete, the two machines link up and are ready to begin swapping files.

That's an extremely powerful feature, and it can save you a lot of grief.

Now, in the latest LapLink Pro version, you can even perform that "cloning" operation over a modem. It will take a few minutes to transfer the program—that's a lot of code to ship over a dial-up phone line at 2,400 bps or even 9,600 bps—but you'll soon be in business. This also means that LapLink has now become an excellent remote-computing program, if all you want to do is retrieve files from your desktop machine when you're away from the office.

It's a mess to crawl around behind a desktop PC to connect, then disconnect a serial cable to make these file transfers. Instead, buy a separate serial cable just for this purpose, plug it into a serial port on your PC, and leave it connected. Run that cable down onto the floor under your desk and forward towards your chair. Leave it on the floor, tucked under a pedestal of your desk or otherwise out of the way.

Then, when you need to make a file-transfer, all you have to do is pick up that cable, plug it into the portable PC, and you're in business.

If you don't have a serial port available on your desktop PC—most come with just two serial ports, COM1 and COM2, and many of us have long since tied up both of those connectors—look at the Hayes "ESP," or Enhanced Serial Port board, which adds two more serial ports, COM3 and COM4, to your machine. COM1 and COM3 cannot be used at the same time, and COM2 and COM4 cannot be used at the same time; but you can find a combination of port assignments that resolves that problem and gives you four points at which to connect serial devices to your PC.

A little-noticed trick available with recent versions of most file-transfer programs can speed up the copying process substantially, and can make the non-availability of serial ports moot. Most file-transfer programs come set up to transfer data between two PCs' serial ports. But they can be reset to operate between parallel ports, which run much faster. While smart file-transfer programs can trick most PC serial ports into running at up to 70,000 – 80,000 bps—the spec sheet will tell you the figure is 115,200, but you'll rarely achieve that—a parallel-port connection can boost the effective transfer speed to twice that or more.

This avoids tying up a serial port on your PC just for file transfers. But if, like most PCs, your machine has just one parallel port, you won't want to lose it, either. See "In the Office," in "LAN Access" later in the book, for information on Xircom's Parallel Port Duplexor, which can magically turn your single parallel port into two parallel ports, one of which can then be dedicated to a file-transfer cable.

If you want to be able to transfer files to others' PCs when you're on the road, without resorting to the floppy-disk shuffle, you'll want to carry a cable with you. Over the years, a number of file-transfer programs have included cables with their programs which have both serial and parallel connectors at each end, and sometimes even both 9-pin and 25-pin serial connectors, so you can cope with whatever you find on that other computer. But these hydra-headed cables are usually thick, heavy, and clumsy to carry.

Travelling Software has recently released a new, lightweight file-transfer cable with all those plug-on options, but with much less weight and bulk than earlier cables. I worried at first that it was *too* light and would soon break; but I've been carrying one for months, and have never had a problem. It's worth tracking this one down if you plan to carry a file-transfer cable with you.

Backing Up

Most of the data lost by PC users goes down the drain from hard-disk failures. Hard disks have gotten a lot sturdier over the past decade, but that's relative: they're still vulnerable to damage from bumps and shocks.

Why, then, do most notebook- and laptop-PC users think their machines are immune to problems like that? Portables lead a far harder life than deskbound machines. We bump them, drop them, toss attache cases holding them into the back seats of cars and the overhead bins on airliners. It's surprising that the hard disks in these machines last as long as they do.

All that makes backing up portables' hard disks even more important than backing up data on desktop PCs. Yet few portable-PC users ever run backups. Here's how to make backups a quick, easy part of your routine.

Floppy Mania

JUST SAY NO.

No matter how many times you hear that backing up a computer's hard disk—any computer's hard disk, not just one in a laptop or notebook PC—to floppy disks makes sense, don't believe it. Backing up to a stack of floppies is a technological anachronism no one should put up with any more.

There is only one advantage to using floppies for hard-disk backups, and it's a highly deceptive one: economy. Because you already own the required floppy-disk drive, this reasoning goes, backing up to floppies must certainly be the most economical of all backup strategies. After all, all you need is a stack of blank floppies, and . . . .

And a LOT of time.

Do a little quick math. Say you've got a 40 MB hard disk in your notebook PC. And say you've used about 35 MB of that space. Now run a full backup of that disk to floppies. Ignoring for the moment the possibility of using a back-up program that provides data-compression as it copies files to floppies, consider how many floppy disks you'll need: about 25. (That's 35 MB of data divided by a maximum of 1.4 MB per floppy. Yes, $3^1/_2$-inch floppy disks formatted under MS-DOS as high-density disks do hold a maximum of 1.44 MB, but backup programs steal some of that space as part of their overhead. You'll do well to net-out 1.4 MB per disk.)

Those 25 floppies aren't all that expensive, by themselves—about $25, probably, if you buy disks at good prices. The real cost is your time, to sit there and shuffle 25 disks in and out of the machine—waiting, of course, with each one, while the data is copied over to it, then taking it out of the machine, labelling it (God forbid you should misnumber one, in the event you ever need to restore that data), then putting the next one in.

Oh, and don't forget about the time required to format the disks. Even if your back-up program automatically detects that disks are unformatted and handles that for you transparently (and almost all of the backup programs you'd want to use do), there's still the additional time required for that formatting.

How long does that take? Despite back-up software vendors' claims of very fast data-transfer rates, and the advantages of incremental formatting as they go along, figure on at least a half-hour every time you back up to formatted disks, an hour if they're not formatted.

So if you buy the argument about backing up to floppies being cheap, then you must put an awfully small value on your time.

Or you just don't plan to make backups very often.

I mentioned a moment ago that some programs compress data on the fly as they write to a backup floppy (or to any other DOS-based backup medium, for that matter). They do, and that means you'll use fewer floppies. That will cut your floppy-disk bill by a little, but overall, it probably won't save all that much time. Because the compression process is not exactly a real-time, zero-cost procedure. If you save 10 percent on the time required to run a complete backup, you're doing well.

Some will complain that I've stacked the deck here by talking only about complete backups—copies of everything on the entire hard disk. Instead, they say, why not make incremental backups—adding to a master set of backup floppies only those files added or changed since the last time you backed up the hard disk?

Wrong, wrong, wrong. Lots of people make incremental backups—or at least, so the backup spoftware vendors will tell you. But that's a lousy way to save time and money: your backup disk-set grows increasingly unwieldy, and a full restore from that set of floppies is really a nightmare. You want every backup to be full and complete, entire unto itself.

Every backup? Of course, you want more than one.

The usual system is to have a set of three rotating full backups, called something like grandfather, father and son. Rather than erasing the last set of back-ups by overwriting those disks with the new set, smart people overwrite only the oldest of those three sets each time they go through the back-up routine. That way, if something goes wrong during the backup process itself—or if, though things seemed to go fine during the backup itself, you later find when you try to run a restore from those disks that they're mysteriously unreadable—you still have a viable, relatively recent set of backup disks.

So let's increase that number of backup floppies you'll have to buy and maintain—again, get the labels right; mix disks from the three sets and you're dead if you need to restore—to about 75 disks. Grouped and sequenced properly, of course.

You say your mother didn't raise you to be a file clerk? Mine, either.

You want a backup system which puts a whole, complete back-up of the contents of your portable PC's hard disk in one place, on one device—a tape cassette, or data cartridge, or DAT cassette, or a Bernoulli or SyQuest hard-disk cartridge, or a partition on your desktop PC's hard disk, or on a second, separate, backups-only hard disk installed in that desktop PC, or on a certain hard disk on one of your network's servers. All of which are discussed elsewhere in this part of the book.

And you want walk-away convenience—the ability to set up the back-up routine, then go to lunch or meeting, or home for the night, certain that it will be completed without any further intervention by you. All of those alternative media offer that, too.

In sum, you want to make backup so easy and foolproof that you'll actually do it, and do it often.

But not, *please*, to floppies.

JUST SAY NO.

Parallel-Port SCSI Connections

There's more to backing up than floppy disks. Digital Audio Tape (DAT) cassettes, 128 MB rewritable optical-disk cartridges, SyQuest cartridges, Bernoulli cartridges, and more offer a world of fast, reliable backup solutions.

Problem is, they all also require installing a Small Computer Systems Interface (SCSI) card in an expansion slot in your PC. And you may have noticed that few laptop PCs, and no notebook PCs I've seen, have ISA or EISA industry-standard expansion-card slots.

But don't give up yet.

In a business full of fascinating and sometimes even worthwhile gadgets and accessories, one of my all-time favorite add-ons is Trantor Corporation's parallel-port MiniSCSI adapter. This tiny, candy-bar-sized adapter plugs into the parallel printer port of your portable PC (or your desktop machine, for that matter), and then gives you back both that standard parallel printer connection and also an industry-standard SCSI connection.

There's no interference whatsoever with the printer hook-up; you can easily keep both a printer and a SCSI device connected to the computer at the same time. Activitating the SCSI port requires only adding a line calling a Trantor-supplied device driver to your CONFIG.SYS file, and copying that little driver program onto your PC's hard disk. The MiniSCSI even draws its power from the SCSI device, so there's no battery to run down, and no "wall wart" power transformer to lose.

Stick a Trantor Mini-SCSI on the back of your portable, and that whole world of SCSI-based backup devices is open to you. To be sure, many of these SCSI-driven backup systems are more suited to use at your desktop than on the road—but that's exactly where most of us run backups, anyway, at our desks. Those of us who make backups at all, that is.

And some SCSI-based backup systems—the tiny magneto-optical 128 MB optical-disk-cartridge drives, for example—are utterly portable, if you want to haul one with you when you travel.

There's a hidden benefit here: if you're willing to carry around that backup system, and it's a random-access device, such as a 128 MB optical drive or a Syquest or Bernoulli drive, you also have in effect a portable external hard disk, which you can use for additional primary storage, over and above that provided by the internal hard disk in your portable PC. (I think the truly tiny external hard disks, such as those from Liberty, which connect to your PC through the plain, unadulterated parallel printer port, make more sense if you mainly need extra storage on the road. But for occasional use, something like the Bernoulli Transportable or any of the many small 128 MB magneto-optical drives are fine.)

If the last chapter didn't persuade you that you really don't want to back up to floppies, maybe the simplicity and speed of this approach will. The Trantor MiniSCSI costs just $179 list, and a lot less at typical street prices. Add the output device of your choice and you have a highly effective, high-performance back-up system—including, in most cases, an external storage system which can also be accessed directly, at your desktop or on the road, for other storage needs.

Finally, if you're interested in carrying lots of reference data with you—or using it at your desk, if you choose the one-PC/one-portable path—note that the MiniSCSI can also be the gateway from your portable PC to the world of CD-ROM drives, all of which work via SCSI connections, and all of which can be easily connected to your laptop or notebook PC through this simple and elegant device.

Backing Up to Your Desktop PC

Often, the simplest answers to a problem lurk right under our noses. We don't need to buy anything or learn anything new to put those answers to work; we just need the *idea.* That's how I'd categorize the notion of backing up a laptop or notebook PC's hard disk to the hard disk of a desktop PC.

(I know, I know—I've argued elsewhere in this book [in "An Adjunct to your Desktop PC . . . Or Your *Only* System?" and in other chapters] that you really don't need both a desktop PC and a notebook or laptop: the latter can serve perfectly well as your sole machine. And so if you've taken my advice, then that desktop machine is long gone. But realistically, most notebook and laptop PC users already have that second machine on their desks . . . and it's not going anywhere anytime soon. I'm not being a hypocrite, just a realist.)

Backing up a portable PC onto a desktop computer's disk is simplicity itself. You set aside a portion of the hard disk on the desktop machine as a "backup zone" for the contents of the portable's hard disk, then periodically copy everything from the notebook to the desktop computer. If you have plenty of space on the desktop PC's disk, you can even set aside two or perhaps three of these backup zones, so you can maintain a rotating set of portable backups. A computer-to-computer file-transfer program such as Travelling Software's LapLink makes the backup easy.

If this notion appeals to you—and I hope it does—I have a few suggestions, and also a warning.

The best way to back up onto your desktop computer is to format that PC's hard disk with one or more partitions, each just big enough for a complete dump of the portable's disk. This kind of multiple-partition hard-disk formatting used to be commonplace—mandatory, actually—because before the advent of MS-DOS version 4.0, DOS couldn't handle disks larger than 32 MB. If you bought an 80 MB, or 150 MB, or 300 MB disk, you first divided it into a series of "logical drives," each (usually) about 32 MB in size. Each logical drive was then given a unique drive name, beginning with C: and running as high as necessary.

For example, the 330 MB hard disk on one of the desktop PCs in my office appears to its user as 10 hard disks, identified as C: through L:. The first nine, C: through K:, are 32 MB drives (actually, 33,431,552 bytes each; the difference arises from our casual and imprecise math when we say "32 MB"), and the last, L:, is 16 MB (actually 16,453,632 bytes). The drive is partitioned that way because it was first set up under DOS 3.1, which didn't support larger partitions, and we've never reformatted it.

Although DOS 4.0 and later releases support much larger, whole-disk partitions, many people, myself included, find managing today's very large hard disks as a series of smaller logical drives easier and more sensible than setting them up as one big drive. Grouping programs according to some personal schema onto those several logical drives—DOS and DOS word-processing applications and their data files on C:, DOS spreadsheets and utilities and *their* data files on D:, Windows plus its utilities and fonts on E:, Windows applications and associated data files on F: through H:, and so on—makes a lot of sense.

That kind of disk structure and related directory structures also makes visualizing, say, logical drive K: as the designated back-up zone for a notebook's hard-disk files much easier.

So if you're setting up a new desktop PC's hard disk, and like this idea of using part of that hard disk for backing up your portable PC, consider setting up one partition of the same size as (or slightly larger than) your portable's hard disk. You might, for example, create on a desktop's 150

MB drive four 32 MB partitions, plus a 20 MB-plus partition for portable backups. (Note that DOS 4.0 and later versions are perfectly happy to support such multiple logical hard-disk partitions; they just don't *require* you to break down a large disk into those logical units.)

If, on the other hand, your desktop PC's hard disk is already formatted as one big partition, then the more logical approach is to just create a new directory—"LAPBACK"?—within that large storage space, as a dedicated backup zone for your travelling machine.

Either way, subsequent portable back-ups are fast and easy. LapLink or another, similar program will copy the entire contents of your portable's disk to that zone quickly and easily. How quickly? I just ran a back-up of the nearly full 20 MB disk in one of the notebook PCs I use to the designated back-up area of the hard disk in a desktop PC here; it took *LapLink* less than 20 minutes. It was a completely unattended process: I hit the a key in LapLink and walked away.

(Making laptop-to-desktop file transfers that quickly and easily requires having copies of LapLink on both machines already, and leaving a cable that's connected to either a serial or parallel port on your desktop machine lying under your desk, so you don't have to wrestle with turning your desktop machine around and unplugging and replugging things, just to make a file transfer. But you should do that anyway, not just for backups; see "File Transfer Utilities" in this section of the book.)

What if you don't have a large enough hard disk on your desktop PC to manage this little trick? Or if you do have a large disk . . . but it's nearly full?

Then consider installing a second, inexpensive hard disk in your desktop machine, *just for portable backups.* These days you can buy very good half-height 20 MB to 40 MB (formatted capacity) hard disks for a song. The world has gone on to bigger hard disks, and these drives—solid, reliable, one-generation-behind units—are going begging. So if one of these older, smaller drives is large enough to hold the entire contents of your portable's hard disk, you could add it to your desktop setup very inexpensively, for cost-effective portable backups.

Alternatively, if you have a low-rise, small-footprint desktop machine, without any open drive bays left, you could plug a Quantum/Plus Development Hardcard or other hard-disk-on-a-card subsystem into one of the expansion slots in your PC, with the same result. As Quantum/Plus has increased its products' storage capacities (to as much as 105 MB in the XL series), and has also increased the operating speed of those disks as well, the older and slower but still entirely satisfactory 20 MB – 40 MB Hardcards can often be found, new in the box, for just $100 – $150.

Hard disks mounted on bus cards are incredibly easy to install, even for the fumble-fingered. Just remove the cover of your desktop PC, push the card into an open expansion slot, and close the lid. You may also have to run a simple INSTALL program, which usually sets up a simple, transparent, performance-boosting cache for the disk.

As slick as backing up a portable to a desktop machine can be, it has one limitation: security. When you back up a notebook's hard disk to tape cartridges, DAT cassettes, or any other external, portable medium, you can stash that backup—or even an extra copy of it—someplace safe from the ravages of fire, forgetfulness, and failure of mechanical devices. But if you're backing up to a hard disk in your desktop machine, then your backup is just as vulnerable as everything else on that machine's hard disk. If the desktop's hard disk fails, your backup may be lost forever.

To be sure, it would be an amazing coincidence if the hard disk in your notebook PC failed, and then when you repaired or replaced that disk and turned to your desktop PC to restore your most recent backup to the notebook's new disk, the disk in the desktop machine suddenly failed, too. But statistics and odds-makers aside, curious things do happen.

Worse, if your desktop and laptop machines are sitting side by side in your office and there's a fire, or water damage—or a break-in by a thief eager to snatch a few high-value items he can quickly fence on the street—then you could lose all your data. There are reasons computer-security people recommend keeping at least one recent set of backups off-site . . . .

So a system that's slick and easy—and one that can usually be put into place without spending a nickel on anything new—may in the end be less secure than you want or need.

My experience, though, is that so few portable-PC owners *ever* back up their hard disks—and I've found the numbers are even worse for notebook owners than among those who use bigger, older portables—that the bigger risk is that unless you adopt a system this cheap and simple, you may never back up at all.

And that, I guarantee, is a prescription for disaster.

Backing Up to the Network

This is a good idea, which nonetheless can get you in a lot of trouble.

One of the slickest of all methods of backing up a laptop or notebook PC's hard disk is by dumping, from time to time, the entire contents of the machine's hard disk over your local-area network to a designated storage space on one of the servers connected to the network.

It's quick to set up, so painless you'll do it frequently, and it doesn't require you to invest a cent in backup media or hardware.

What *can* get you in trouble is your network manager's reaction to the idea. So make sure he or she agrees that it's a good approach for you, and helps you set up the process, lest you anger someone you really want as a friend and ally.

Network managers are a beleaguered lot. They worry constantly about the network going down, and when it does—which is inevitable—the whole world comes down on them with demands to get it back up, fast, no matter what. They worry about having not enough storage capacity on the LAN's servers, about whether LAN traffic is becoming too heavy, about users who may be running illegal copies of programs and storing them on "their" server, about viruses infecting the network operating system or the applications stored on the servers, about . . . .

The list is almost endless.

So then you come along, proposing to this worried person that he or she set aside a space of 40 MB, 60 MB, or whatever the capacity of your portable PC's hard disk, on one of the hard disks in one of the servers on the network. For your exclusive use, of course. And furthermore, you want to load up the network with the traffic involved in shipping 40 MB or 60 MB of data down to that server from time to time. (Of course, should your portable PC's hard disk ever fail, then you'll also want to tie up the net by *uploading* that data from the server back to the portable's disk.)

Ask some network managers about that, and they'll hand you your head.

Ask others, and they'll think for a minute, then tell you it's a great idea.

This is classic Theory X/Theory Y management-thinking at work. Some network managers hold the view that they are the guardians and protectors of the network against all comers, especially those damned users who want to store things on it and ship files and back and forth. The company hired them to keep that network up and running, and by God, that's exactly what they're going to do. Even if to do so they have to keep users off the thing.

Others view themselves as facilitators, people who are supposed to make network users' lives easier. Anything they can reasonably do to make that happen is welcome news to them: that's why they're there. And backups . . . well, every PC manager of every stripe knows users don't make backups nearly often enough, so anyone who wants help setting up a nifty backup system ought to get priority help.

Which kind of person manages *your* network?

In truth, of course, most network managers fall somewhere in the middle, and many more of them are near the second pole than the first. If you're lucky enough to have the second kind of network manager, he or she will find you that space on a server, show you how to map to it, set up access privileges that keep others from accidentally destroying your backed-up data, and show you how to copy the disk to the network when you want to run backups. He or she might even write a simple batch file to automate the process for you, and then copy that file to your portable PC's disk, or install on your portable a backup program to handle the task.

He's likely to ask you to please make backups only at night, when network traffic is slow, rather than clogging up the always-too-limited bandwidth on the network during the business day. Great. Set it up to run when you go home in the evening; when you come back in the morning, the job will be done.

I'm always amazed at the sharp division between kinds of network managers when I suggest this notion to them. Some absolutely love it, and see it as a way to help their users perform a critical function. (Because they already back up their servers' files automatically, they know they've taken care of most of the backup needs of the desktop-PC users in the office. But conscientious network managers worry, too, about how their PC users with portables are going to back up their files; here, they find a way to do it.)

Others become apoplectic, telling me I'm crazy and that I'm trying to undermine the integrity of their operations.

What if EVERYone did that? they cry.

Well, if everyone did it, (a) they'd have to add more network capacity, but (b) their users would no longer be plagued with lost-data problems when their portables' disks crash. The company would run more smoothly, and laptop and notebook PC users in the company would be more productive.

Is that so bad?

LAN Access

Cutting the cord to the office local-area network is a painful step for some PC users. It's easy to get used to all that data, all those programs, and all those peripheral resources available through the network. Just log-on, and you're in business.

Too often, though, portable PCs become like islands, cut off from those resources—in other words, NOT in business.

Here's how to make connecting to your network easy, whether you're logging-on in the office or from across the country.

In the Office

If your office has a local-area network connecting its PCs, printers, and other devices, you'll want to make sure your laptop or notebook PC has ready access to that network. If you still use separate portable and desktop PCs, access to the LAN provides an easy path to transferring files to and from your portable. And it's absolutely critical if you plan to use the portable PC as your *only* PC: if your PC is cut off from the network, you're out of business.

Some laptop PCs have room for a half-length or (rarely) full-length expansion card. If so, you can connect your laptop to the network with the same kind of LAN adapter used on the desktop PCs in your office. There are no serious differences in connecting a laptop and a desktop via expansion-slot adapter cards; your LAN administrator will help you get connected.

If, as is probably the case, your laptop or notebook doesn't have room for a conventional network adapter card, then you'll have to use one of the several kinds of external LAN adapters made especially for portable PCs. This is hardly a burden; indeed, I often use these "pocket LAN adapters" for quick connection of standard desktop PCs to LANs, because they're so fast and easy to set up.

There are two modest drawbacks to using pocket LAN adapters. First is performance: because (with one exception) pocket adapters connect through the computer's parallel printer port, they operate somewhat more slowly than internal adapter cards, which plug directly into a computer's expansion bus. And if your portable has an older-style one-way parallel port, as opposed to a bidirectional port, they'll run somewhat slower still. But either way, the performance penalty is modest; most users will never notice the difference.

Pocket LAN adapters also cost more than conventional LAN adapter cards. These days you can buy a decent 16-bit Arcnet or Ethernet card for $175–$250; pocket LAN adapters for Arcnet and Ethernet networks list for $400–$500, and typically sell for $300–$400. (Token Ring adapter cards and pocket adapters usually cost about $200–$300 more than Ethernet and Arcnet connections.)

That price difference is more than offset, most network managers would agree, by the pocket adapters' quick installation and setup time—and even more by the convenience of being able to finally bring portable PCs in as full partners on the network.

The pocket LAN adapter business was invented by Xircom, which now has a wide line of second-generation pocket adapters. Xircom units can connect to Ethernet, Token Ring and Arcnet-based networks in the most common combinations of wiring types (thick or thin Ethernet coax, shielded or unshielded twisted-pair). I've used Xircom adapters for years, with great success. With the latest Series II adapters, Xircom has achieved a level of compatibility, reliability, and performance that is unmatched in the pocket-adapter business.

That said, corporate clients of mine have also had success with pocket LAN adapters from Solectek and D-Link, and there are other vendors in the market, too.

A special class of pocket LAN adapters comes from Salt Lake's Megahertz Corp., formerly best known for portable PC modems. Megahertz produces a line of pocket adapters for Toshiba portable PCs which bypass the parallel port and instead plug directly into the proprietary bus slot found on some Toshiba models. Because they have direct access to the bus, they perform on the same level as internal adapter cards in desktop PCs.

Note, however, that performance isn't only a matter of bus versus parallel port connections. It also depends on the quality of the network-driver software provided with the pocket adapter. In my experience, Xircom's drivers are also superior to those of its competition, with faster performance and glitch-free setup.

Despite their apparently portable nature, most pocket LAN adapters never leave their owners' desks. It's certainly possible to carry one along with you as you travel, so you can plug into networks wherever you go. But remember that these devices are precisely matched to specific network topologies and cabling schemes, so unless your adapter exactly matches the topology and cabling of the network to which you hope to connect, it won't work.

If you frequently travel to a few of your company's field offices, all of which use the same kind of network and cabling you have in your office, you're in luck: bring along your pocket adapter, plug in, and go to work. Otherwise, call ahead to make sure you know what you'll be connecting to.

It would be possible to put together a kit of, say, all of the different Xircom models, and carry that kit with you when you travel to make sure you could connect to almost any LAN you found. No doubt someone, somewhere, actually does that—but it's a bizarre and expensive scheme, and not one you're likely to adopt.

If you do come to rely on a pocket LAN adapter, let me tell you about a wonderful and little-known tool you may find invaluable.

Once that pocket LAN adapter is connected to your portable PC's parallel printer port, of course, there's no way to connect a printer directly to the computer. That's usually not a problem, because one of the primary reasons for connecting to the network is to gain access to the shared printers on the LAN. But many of us grow tired of running down the hall to distant network printers all the time, and thus cadge a separate, personal printer for our own offices. These so-called "local" printers aren't on the network—they're just for our own use—and so they have to plug into the PC's printer connector.

But with a pocket LAN adapter in place, you don't *have* a printer port anymore.

Xircom to the rescue once again. The company's little-known $100 wonder, the Xircom Parallel Port Duplexor, turns your notebook or laptop PC's one parallel printer port into two. Driver software makes each port separately addressable. The local printer's cable plugs into one of the connectors on the Duplexor; the pocket LAN adapter plugs into the other.

You're on the network, and your local printer is also on line, too. Slick, fast, and foolproof.

Just don't tell everyone in the office about this trick, or they'll all want local printers, too. And suddenly your friendly network manager won't be so friendly any more.

On the Road

Most local-area networks have "dial-out" capability. That is, somewhere on the network there is some form of modem pooling which allows PC users connected to the LAN to place data calls through those shared modems to online data services, external e-mail systems, and other off-premises resources.

Far fewer networks, however, have "dial-*in*" access, which allows users with proper access privileges to call in from their portable PCs, log on, and use the network's resources. That's silly, and reflects both an obsolete view of network security in general and also a perspective on how businesspeople use computers and networks that's decidedly behind the times.

The security argument is at first serious, and maybe even scary: open up your LAN to dial-in access and you open up the network, and every device and storage system connected to it to the predators we call hackers. Just as mainframe computer systems are sometimes illegally entered by hackers who've broken the code, so to speak, for remote access, LANs too can be vulnerable to unauthorized entry by techno-snoops.

It's not wrong to be aware of this problem, nor even to be concerned about the dangers. It *is* wrong to act as if there are no defenses against unauthorized access, and as if legitimate users' access isn't worth the trouble of resolving the security issues. There are any number of simple and effective security techniques and products available to control off-premises LAN access through dial-in connections; tell your network administrator to get up to speed on the tools of his or her profession.

On the second problem—network administrators' failure to understand just how important network access is for travelling workers who rely on their portable PCs—you'll probably need to do a little evangelizing. While it's evident to you and to me that what we do on our laptop or notebook PCs away from the office is just as important as what we do at our desks—and sometimes, far more important—some network managers still see portable PCs as little more than notetakers and toys. Why would they need to be connected to the almighty network?

That's tough to overcome, but until you do so, you won't get far in persuading him or her to install the necessary tools to allow remote access to the LAN.

A description and analysis of remote-access network software is beyond the scope of this book. Briefly, Novell, the largest supplier of business networking software, has recently introduced extremely good new software add-ons for dial-in access. Where once dialing into a Novell Netware network was a swamp, and network managers had to cope with a narrow range of generally inadequate third-party tools, now Novell's own offerings allow easy, secure dial-in.

Artisoft, whose LANtastic software holds as strong a position at the small-network end of the market as Novell's Netware does at the top, also has introduced improved dial-in products.

For three years I've been telling network managers in columns and in speeches at meetings and trade shows that if their networks don't have dial-in, they don't have real networks. I often irritate them with that line, but enough come 'round afterwards to tell me they agree—even if they haven't implemented dial-in access on *their* networks just yet—that it's clear they understand the problem.

Remember the line about the squeaky wheel getting the grease?

RESOURCES

Where to Find It . . .

While it's easy enough to find a copy of 1-2-3 or a LaserJet III printer, many good personal computer tools are devilishly difficult to find. Their manufacturers often have thin to virtually nonexistent distribution, they believe they can't afford to advertise in the computer magazines, and computer resellers have never heard of the stuff.

In this book I've referred to many of these obscure but useful little products. Here's a guide to contacting the vendors of every product mentioned in the book. Good luck on your search!

1-2-3
Lotus Develop. Corp.
617-693-8600

386/Max
Qualitas
302-469-8848

Brooklyn Bridge
5th Generation Systems
800-373-4384

Canon printers
Canon USA
516-488-6700

Carbon Copy Plus
Microcom
617-551-1000

Citizen printers
Citizen America
310-453-0614

CloseUp
Norton-Lambert
805-964-6767

CO/Session
Triton Technology
201-855-9608

Compaq computers
Compaq Corp.
713-370-0670

CompuAdd computers
CompuAdd Corp.
800-531-5475

Compushield cases
Solidex, Inc.
714-599-2666

CP+ Connection
CP+
800-274-4277

Dell computers
Dell Corp.
512-338-4400

Diconix printers
Kodak
312-218-5305

EyeRelief
SkiSoft
617-863-1876

Fast Lynx
Rupp Technologies
602-244-9922

Flashdrive hard disks
BSE Electronics
714-258-8722

Genovation keypads
Genovation, Inc.
714-833-3355

Harvard Graphics
Software Publ. Corp.
800-345-2888

Hot Line 2
Smith Micro
714-964-0412

Hot Wire
Data Storm Technol.
341-443-3282

Konnex box
Unlimited Systems
800-275-6354

LapLink Pro
Travelling Software
206-483-8088

Laptop UltraVision
Personics
508-897-1575

Logitech mice
Logitech, Inc.
800-231-7717

Magellan
Lotus Develop. Corp.
617-693-8600

Mannesmann printers
Mannesmann Tally
206-251-5524

Megahertz adapters
Megahertz Corp.
800-527-8677

Microcom modems
Microcom
617-555-1000

Microsoft Excel
Microsoft Corp.
206-882-8080

Microsoft Windows
Microsoft Corp.
206-882-8080

Microsoft Word
Microsoft Corp.
206-882-8080

Mitsubishi fax modems
Mitsubishi Intl.
708-860-4200

NEC PCs, CD-ROMs
NEC America
508-264-8000

Norton Utilities
Symantec Corp.
408-253-9600

Q&A
Symantec Corp.
408-253-9600

QBlazer modem
Telebit Corp.
800-835-3248

QEMM-386
Quarterdeck Software
212-392-9701

Seikosha printers
Seikosha America
201-327-7227

Sharp computers
Sharp Electronics
201-529-9600

Solectek adapters
Solectek Corp.
619-450-1220

Stacker 2.0
Stac Electronics
800-522-7822

Super PC-Kwik
Multisoft
503-642-7108

Targus cases
Targus, Inc.
714-523-5429

TI computers
Texas Instruments
800-527-3500

Toshiba computers
Toshiba America
714-583-3000

WordPerfect
WordPerfect Corp.
901-225-5000

Xircom adapters
Xircom Corp.
818-878-7600

Zenith computers
Zenith Data Systs.
800-523-9393

INDEX

A

B

C

E

F

G

H

M

Q

R

S

T

W

X

Y

Z